THE GREAT OUTDOORS BOOK

OF

FLORIDA SNAKES

D1446425

Cover illustration: Southern black racer and eastern coral snake.

THE GREAT OUTDOORS BOOK OF

FLORIDA
SNAKES

By Robert Anderson

Edited by Joyce Allyn

Photos and illustrations by the author

 A Great Outdoors Book

Great Outdoors Publishing Company
4747 28th Street North
St. Petersburg, FL 33714
Publishers & Booksellers

Printed in the United States of America
on recycled paper

CONTENTS

INTRODUCTION

The purpose of this book is to introduce to the reader the common snakes, poisonous and non-poisonous, that live and breed in the state of Florida.

It is assumed that the general reader of this book is not a trained herpetologist, but a nonprofessional person who is interested in learning more about some of the other creatures with whom we share our planet. Toward that end, the author attempts to present in nontechnical language a condensed body of interesting (but scientifically accurate) information about one small group of creatures inhabiting this one small geographic section of the planet – that is, the snakes of Florida.

This is not to say that no scientific terms are used; some anatomical names are in fact employed, in the belief that learning them might prove helpful to anyone who wishes to pursue more detailed (and technical) information. Any book of this size can, of course, offer only a tiny fraction of the immense body of information that exists on the general subject of snakes, and which is available in an overwhelming number of volumes.

So the narrower view of this book is to fine-tune some of that vast sea of knowledge, choosing only that pertinent to this one region, for the benefit of those who have neither the time nor the inclination to sift through mountains of facts.

However, the book has other goals: Snakes are wild animals, and as such are to be feared no more nor less than many others. Many people fear and dislike all snakes because they have never allowed themselves to learn about them, nor to see that many of them are among the beautiful and beneficial creatures of the world. It is hoped that understanding, familiarity, and recognition, may dispel some myths and lead to a greater appreciation of these animals whose world it was, before it was ours!

This book does repudiate some myths, and presents some facts from which the reader can draw his own conclusions regarding other possible misconceptions. A large part of the book, however, is devoted to recognition – identification. Text, descriptions, and illustrations were chosen for that purpose. Accurate identification is of prime importance for two reasons. One, the protection of people, requires no further explanation. (Don't pick up a coral snake. Coral snakes are dangerous.) Two, the protection of snakes. (Don't kill a kingsnake just because it looks like a coral snake.) But in order to know which "not to pick up" and which "not to kill" you must be able to identify each.

Snakes are a link in the food chain, and each link in a chain is important. Many snakes are invaluable to man in keeping insects and rodents at bay. (The little ringneck snake you killed in the garden may have been busily ridding your yard of the termites that were ready to invade your house).

But aside from that, snakes are simply part of our inherited wild life, in an environment that further deteriorates daily at the hands of humanity. Surely we need not declare war on creatures that are beautiful, helpful and, if not molested, non-threatening. After all, those words describe some nonpoisonous snakes more accurately than they describe some members of the human race!

2

THE LIFE HISTORY OF SNAKES

Snakes, along with lizards, are by far the most numerous and diverse of modern reptiles. A single species of *Sphenodon*, the lizardlike reptile of New Zealand, known commonly as the tuatara, is but a single species in its animal order, truly a living fossil. About 25 species of crocodilians (crocodiles, alligators and gavials), some 400 species of turtles, possibly 3800 species of lizards and about 3000 species of snakes are distributed throughout the world.

Snakes belong to the suborder Serpentes, and are placed in the animal order Squamata. This order also includes the lizards, which belong to the suborder Sauria. It is very likely that this great group of Squamata, among the reptiles, has prevailed since the Age of Dinosaurs. However, the snakes, according to fossil evidence, were the last of all reptiles to develop, and are believed to be in essence highly modified lizards. Unfortunately the fossil history of snakes is very fragmentary; therefore it is largely through comparative anatomy of modern forms that we can make an "educated guess" regarding their progress through the ages. Snakes are believed to have evolved from burrowing lizards. A group of long-legged, short-bodied lizard forms is thought to have gone through a transition that eventually produced primitive snakes, bulky serpents related to modern boas and pythons which still retain traces of legs. Snakes first appeared in the upper Cretaceous period 80 million years ago.

3

Lizards are known from the upper Jurassic period about 130 million years ago.

Unlike lizards, snakes lack legs, movable eyelids, external ear openings, eardrums, and middle ear cavities. Also, the two halves of their lower jaw are joined by a ligament at the chin. However, no single feature is unique to snakes or lizards. Many lizards, for example, do not have legs, and some also lack ears; some snakes have stubs of hind legs or, internally, the bony girdle for their attachment.

SNAKES – IN GENERAL

Snakes are ectothermic (cold-blooded) animals, which means that their body temperature is regulated by the temperature of the surrounding environment. There are limits beyond which a snake will not voluntarily allow its body temperature to drop or to rise. Temperatures too high or too low can cause the death of a snake. Most snakes have an active body temperature of between 80 and 100 degrees Fahrenheit. When the outside temperature begins to rise above a snake's desired range, the snake will seek the cooler shelter of the underbrush, a deep shadow of a log, or creep under rocks or debris of almost any kind. They often appropriate the abandoned burrows of other animals; the burrows dug by gopher tortoises seem to be a favorite shelter, not only of snakes, but all kinds of animals. In cold climates, should the outside temperature drop too low, a snake will go into hibernation by retreating deep into a woody or rocky crevice for the duration of the cold weather. Hibernation is a sort of suspended animation in which the reptile's body temperature drops below that of the active state, and the heartbeat and respiration almost cease.

Upon first seeing a snake it might be natural to feel a little sorry for a creature that is without arms or legs – a condition which would appear to be a most discouraging handicap in the eternal struggle for survival. In reality, however, a snake needs no

5

sympathy, for it has developed some highly complex structures in compensation, making it the most successful of all the reptiles living today.

All snakes are limbless and most have long, slender, almost cylindrical bodies. The bodies of all snakes are completely covered with scales, a most useful identification feature. In some groups the scales of the head are small; in others they are large and irregular in size. Scales on the lower (belly) surfaces are called ventral scales, plates or scutes, and are usually wide. The scales on the upper surfaces are called dorsal scales and are usually smaller. There are exceptions in which all the scales over the body are small, like those of the worm snakes

DORSAL (top) VIEW
(Snake)

Smooth scales   Keeled scales   Head plates

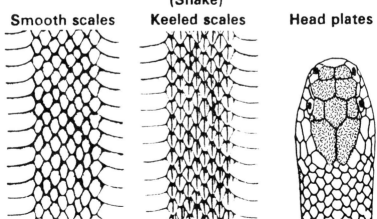

or wart snakes. In most snakes the scales in each row alternate with scales in adjacent rows. The number of scale rows varies from 13 to 150. In snakes with tapered bodies, the number of scale rows decreases toward both the head and tail. In those with cylindrical bodies, such as the coral snakes, the number is the same throughout the length of the body.

VENTRAL (bottom) VIEW
(Snake)

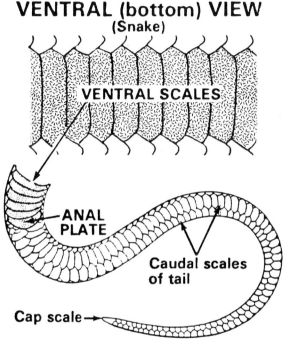

Scales under the tail are called caudal scales. They may occur in two rows (divided), or may be broad like the ventral scales (undivided or entire). The number is often important in identifying related species. A small cone-shaped scale caps the end of the tail. This cap is in no way associated with poison nor is it ever used as a spine or spur in combat.

Dorsal scales on both body and tail may be smooth or may have a median, longitudinal ridge called a keel, in which case they are referred to as keeled scales. The free edge may be rounded or notched and

7

in some kinds of snakes each scale bears two pits or touch-sensitive organs. These are visible only with the aid of a magnifying glass.

Male and female snakes usually look alike. In only a few species is there a notable difference between male and female in either pattern or color. However, males almost always have a longer tail and more caudal scales than do females of the same length. Females usually have a longer body and more ventral plates or scales. However, as a rule, the total number of scales is the same in both sexes of the same species. In some groups, such as the water snakes, there are numerous tiny pits on the scales beneath the male's head. These are the openings to glands that secrete a substance believed to be attractive to the females of the species. In courtship, a male rubs his chin along the female's body. (Some female Madagascar racers have a scaly projection on the snout; this too, may be used in courtship.)

Snakes feed almost exclusively on living animals or eggs. A few kinds will eat dead animals, or can be trained to do so in captivity. A snake catches its food with its mouth, then swallows it whole. Its loosely hung jaws and flexible skin make it possible for a snake to swallow an animal much larger in diameter than that of its own body. Most start swallowing prey as soon as it is captured, often with the victim still struggling; sometimes the struggling continues even in the snake's gullet. If the prey is an animal such as a horned lizard or a catfish, spines can puncture the snake's body wall, and in most cases this proves fatal to the snake. Some snakes use their bodies to hold down struggling prey until they are able to begin the swallowing process. Other snakes, called "constrictors", will hold the live prey in their mouths while tightening their body coils around the body of the prey; only when the victim has succumbed to suffocation does the swallowing process begin. Other snakes have their own specialized methods for killing prey by the injection of venom, a modified saliva which contains protein poison. The venom is secreted by large venom glands which are located in the snake's upper jaw, immediately behind the eyes. The venom is injected into the prey through large, hollow or grooved teeth (fangs) which may be positioned either at the anterior end of the maxillary bone (jaw bone) or, in the rear-fanged snakes, at the

SKULL OF VIPER – RETRACTABLE FANGS
(Rattlesnake)

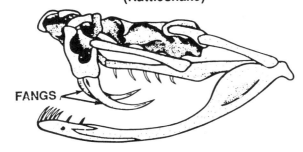

FANGS

SKULL OF RIGID FANGED SNAKE
(Coral snake)

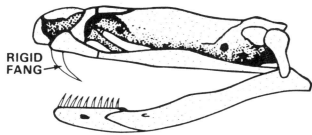

RIGID FANG

REAR-FANGED SNAKE
(Rigid fangs)

VENOM GLAND

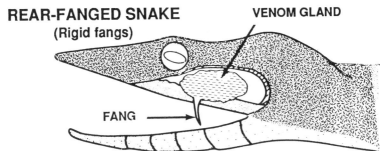

FANG

posterior end of the maxillary bone. Snake venoms affect prey in different ways. Viper venoms affect the blood system (haematoxic), while some others affect the nervous system (neurotoxic).

One way that we classify snakes is by the way the young are produced; some are said to be oviparous (egg laying) while others are ovoviviparous (producing live offspring). Both these terms imply birth from eggs; in the former method the eggs are laid and the offspring develop outside the mother's body, emerging from the eggs weeks later. In ovoviviparous production, the entire development takes place while the eggs are still in the mother's body and the babies leave the maternal body only as they hatch. Thus, although they are "born live", they receive no sustenance from the mother while developing. They were in no way attached to the mother, as young mammals are attached by means of a placenta. The term for this kind of live birth is viviparous. However the term is sometimes used to indicate any live birth, whether ovoviviparous or placental. In almost too small a number of species to mention, a primitive placenta does connect the embryo to the mother snake; this is rare and occurs primarily in snakes which reside in colder climates. Broods or clutches range from three or four to as many as 100. By whatever method they develop, the young are born independent. They receive no parental care. Small snakes mature in about one or two years, while large snakes mature in five or six years; however, growth usually continues throughout the life of a snake.

Snakes find their prey in various ways, but among the most effective structures used by a snake are the pit organs of the pit vipers and some boas. These pits are very sensitive heat detectors, and with these nocturnal (night) snakes can detect prey at a distance.

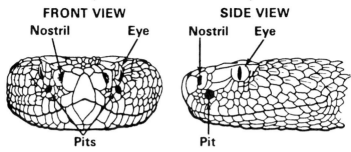

PIT VIPER
(Diamondback rattlesnake)

FRONT VIEW

Nostril   Eye

Pits

SIDE VIEW

Nostril   Eye

Pit

Snakes do not have good vision but even slight movements attract their attention. In fact, most snakes rely largely on movement to find their prey. The snake's tongue plays a very important role. All snakes have forked tongues. When used in conjunction with the Jacobson's organ, the tongue records chemical stimuli for both taste and smell. Most sluggish snakes depend almost exclusively on scent. A water snake will try to swallow anything – even itself – if smeared with the odorous secretion of a frog or a fish.

SENSE OF SMELL
(Snake)

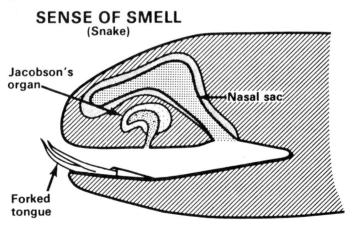

Jacobson's organ

Nasal sac

Forked tongue

Jacobson's organ is used in conjunction with the tongue for recording chemical stimuli for taste and smell.

11

Snakes shed the outer dead skin at least once, and often three or four times, a year. The number of times a snake sheds depends on the species, geographic location, and its physical condition, not on its rate of growth. An injury to the skin may also stimulate more frequent shedding. The cast skin (slough) is turned back at the tip of the snout and pushed off the body wrong side out. Snakes rub against rocks or other objects to help get the skin off.

Snakes move by one of four different methods or a combination of these methods. Most commonly they wiggle their bodies back and forth in S-shaped waves that start at the front end of the body and move to the rear. The body is pushed forward whenever it catches on irregularities on the surface. On a smooth surface snakes can move only very slowly by this "serpentine" movement. The "concertina" method, next most frequently used, involves hitching one part of the body forward in loops while the remainder of the body remains anchored; "rectilinear" locomotion is possible only in such

SNAKE LOCOMOTION

Vertebra

Rib

Superior muscles

Muscles that pulls the body forward

Scale muscles

Ventral scale

heavy bodied snakes as vipers, which have very large
ventral scales. The body moves forward very slowly

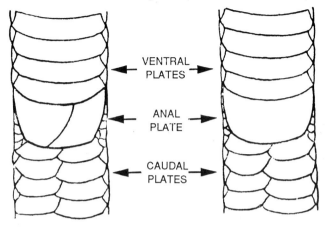

VENTRAL
PLATES

ANAL
PLATE

CAUDAL
PLATES

Anal plate divided (left). Anal plate single (right).

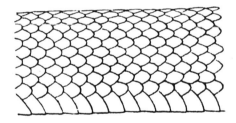

in a straight line, as the ventral scales move in waves
over the ends of the ribs. Amazing, and rarest of all,
is the "sidewinding" locomotion of the horned viper of
North Africa and our horned rattlesnake or
sidewinder of southwestern North America. Both of
these snakes live in loose, shifting sands where other
types of locomotion would not be possible.

13

There are many mistaken beliefs about snakes. Here are some of the facts. Snakes do not charm or hypnotize enemies or prey. No snake can roll like a hoop, and none can blow poisonous vapor. No snake can "sting" with its tail, nor does any snake have a poisonous tongue. Snakes never milk cows. Mother (or father) snakes never swallow their young to protect them. No snake can break into pieces, and no snake's tail can be used like a whip. Snakes do not wait for sundown to die.

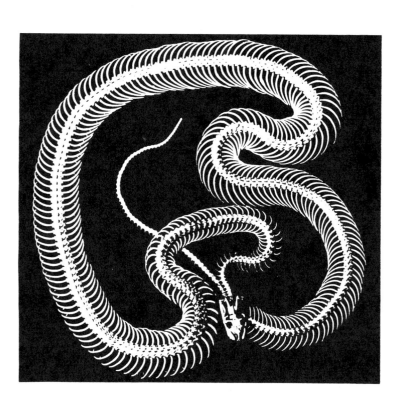

Snake skeleton. Snakes have more ribs than any other animal. Some species have 100, others as many as 400. Displayed above is a South American boa constrictor.

FLORIDA SNAKES

At the present time there are, according to some authorities, a total of sixty different species of snakes that are permanent residents of the Sunshine State. However, a recent checklist, a 1989 release by the Nongame Program of the Florida Game and Fresh Water Fish Commission, lists a total of 68 species. They list seven poisonous plus 61 nonpoisonous species, with the greatest variety residing in the northern part of the state. As one progresses southward, fewer varieties are encountered.

Snakes inhabit all parts of the Sunshine State with at least a few species being found in each of the state's 67 counties. As a guide for locating the range of each species, a map showing Florida's counties is shown on pages 22-23. Snakes live in forests and fields throughout the state, and those called water snakes occupy the many square miles of wetland areas as well as the many freshwater lakes and rivers. Many species of snakes can also be found along the saltwater coasts of both the Atlantic Ocean and the Gulf of Mexico. Some snakes venture far south into the Keys.

The majority of Florida snakes lead a terrestrial life (living upon the ground) while some live in and among the branches of low trees and bushes, and are capable of moving through the interlocking branches with much speed and grace. However Florida is entirely free of tree-dwelling poisonous snakes. Many snakes lead a semi-aquatic life, and live for a great part of their lives in a fresh or saltwater habitat; most are expert swimmers and divers, and some are capable of capturing swimming fish. Some other semi-aquatic species prefer the saltwater marshlands that border our seashores, and a few poisonous species termed "marine snakes" swim in the offshore waters of the state. And last, (and perhaps least but not necessarily fewest) are some small snakes that prefer a subterranean life burrowing beneath the ground, very much like the earthworms.

Florida snakes range in size from the small, ten inch long, fully grown worm snake to the nine foot eastern coachwhip and the equally long indigo snake; most of the snakes of Florida are nonpoisonous. Of the poisonous snakes, the dusky pygmy rattler is the smallest, and the eastern diamondback rattlesnake the largest.

A LARGE CLAN —
THE COLUBRIDAE FAMILY

The family Colubridae is by far the largest of all snake families. Encompassed in this family are approximately 80 percent of all species of snakes distributed around the world. Except for Australia, where the family Elapidae (cobras, coral snakes, etc.) are more numerous, colubrid snakes predominate on all continents. In Florida, nearly all snakes belong to this large family. The only exceptions are the seven hollow-fanged poisonous members and the single member of the blind snake family Typhlopidae. However, some colubrids are poisonous, but in these, the fangs are positioned toward the rear of the upper jaw and are only slightly enlarged. The venom, which is generally mild, flows along a groove in the front of each fang, and into the bite wound. This method of injecting venom is slow, so poisonous colubrids usually have to hold onto their prey for half an hour or more for the venom to take effect. The poison of these rear-fanged snakes primarily affects the nervous system of the prey, and may cause very little swelling.

The Texas lyre snake and the northern cat-eyed snake are rear fanged colubrid snakes from the southwestern United States. None are really dangerous to humans. However, the cat-eyed species is large enough that if a person's finger came in contact with the fangs, it could cause him trouble.

No such accident has appeared on any snake bite record. In other parts of the world there are some rear-fanged snakes of the colubrid family which are considered very dangerous to humans. The boomslang of South Africa is the most dangerous of the colubrid family. It is one of the few deadly poisonous snakes that have fangs in the rear of the upper jaw. The venom of the boomslang acts primarily on the blood and blood vessels, breaking down cells and causing victims to die from a lack of oxygen. Among deaths caused by this species is that of one of the world's famous herpetologists, Karl P. Schmidt.

In Florida there are six species of rear fanged snakes; however all are very small, and their venom very mild. They offer no threat to humans (see crowned snakes, page 115).

NONPOISONOUS SNAKES
(Nonvenomous Snakes)

The majority of Florida snakes are referred to as harmless or nonpoisonous snakes. This author prefers the latter description because very few snakes are entirely harmless to humans. Many so-called harmless snakes have their upper, or lower, or both jaws armed with many sharply pointed teeth, and most of these snakes are capable of delivering a vicious bite that can inflict serious skin punctures and lacerations which if not treated with a good antiseptic could cause serious infections. A serious snake bite (one that is lacerated and bleeds profusely) should be treated like any other bite from a vicious animal.

A nonpoisonous snake is any species that lacks venom glands and fangs for injection into the wound of the victim.

The So-called "Harmless" Snakes

Any time a snake is caught, killed, or seen, and a question arises as to its poisonous versus harmless nature, a presumption of "guilt" is most frequently the verdict. Even educated people, unless specifically knowledgeable, seem unwilling to concede the innocence of the accused snake without the most incontrovertible proof. And then, even in the face of expert testimony to the contrary, there is usually someone in the crowd who recalls a case of serious poisoning from the bite of "this very kind of snake". Actually, among the uninitiated, misidentification of a species is all too common. If this were the case, the remembered bite and subsequent poisoning may well have been inflicted by an entirely different breed of snake.

The expert on the scene could not contradict the accuracy of the report; he can identify the snake before him, but not having seen the snake in the reported, previous incident, he could not identify it. He could, however, point out that very dire consequences often follow the bites of other animals which are unquestionably "nonpoisonous" in the generally accepted usage of the word. He might cite Livingston's statement that the bite of large felines is commonly followed by symptoms of poisoning; also he could likely recall cases of swelling, serious inflammation or perhaps even death which were undoubtedly caused by the bite of rats, dogs, cats, cows, horses, and even man himself.

It should be clear then, that we cannot always conclude that a snake is a venomous kind just because its bite causes symptoms of poisoning.

Nobody today doubts the existence of those minute organisms called bacteria; science shows that bacteria, present in the saliva of every animal, can cause trouble when introduced through the creature's bite. The general public calls these cases "blood poisoning". The professional person refers to them as cases of septicaemia.

The fact that the poison (venom) of snakes is indeed a modified saliva should not lead anyone to suppose that snake venom and bacteria-infected saliva have anything in common – except that either could, in fact, produce fatal results. The medical practitioner must understand the difference and act accordingly; the sooner the general public also understands – and acts accordingly – the better.

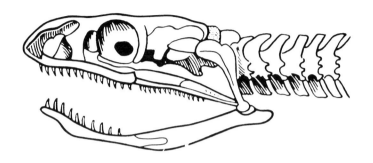

Skull of nonpoisonous snake.

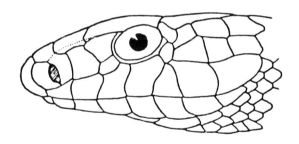

Head of nonpoisonous snake.

FLORIDA COUNTY INDEX MAP

Florida Counties

29	Alachua	42	Hernando	47	Polk
26	Baker	55	Highlands	34	Putnam
7	Bay	46	Hillsborough	33	St. Johns
28	Bradford	5	Holmes	57	St. Lucie
49	Brevard	50	Indian River	2	Santa Rosa
65	Broward	8	Jackson	52	Sarasota
9	Calhoun	16	Jefferson	41	Seminole
58	Charlotte	21	Lafayette	38	Sumter
36	Citrus	39	Lake	20	Suwanee
32	Clay	61	Lee	18	Taylor
64	Collier	14	Leon	27	Union
23	Columbia	25	Levy	40	Volusia
67	Dade	11	Liberty	15	Wakulla
54	DeSoto	17	Madison	4	Walton
22	Dixie	51	Manatee	6	Washington
31	Duval	36	Marion		
1	Escambia	60	Martin		
35	Flagler	66	Monroe		
12	Franklin	30	Nassau		
3	Gadsden	3	Okaloosa		
24	Gilchrist	56	Okeechobee		
59	Glades	44	Orange		
10	Gulf	48	Osceola		
19	Hamilton	63	Palm Beach		
53	Hardee	43	Pasco		
62	Hendry	45	Pinellas		

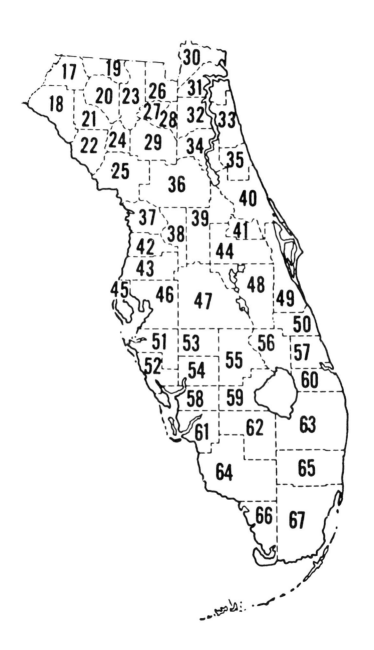

RACERS – Genus *Coluber*

The snakes referred to as "racers" are all slender and graceful snakes, and all are very rapid in their movements. Snakes in this group have a wide distribution, inhabiting North America, Mexico, South and Central America and much of the Eastern Hemisphere. All of the North American species have smooth scales, and although the bodies of all racers appear powerful enough, none of these snakes ever subdue their prey by constriction. Among the racers are some of the fastest crawling snakes, hence the name. The racers of North America are not striking in their coloration, displaying hues of olive, brown or black, but their large size and glossy scales present them as rather showy among colubrid snakes.

There are three species of racers that inhabit the state of Florida.

SOUTHERN BLACK RACER
Coluber constrictor priapus

A long, slender, satiny, smooth-scaled black snake. A very active snake with a very long tail.

Coloration: Uniform black above with satiny luster. Throat and variable expanse of the undersides are usually white. Eyes may be brown or red. Average length is three feet. This snake will defend itself viciously when cornered or handled; when it bites it usually inflicts many skin punctures and lacerations.

The black racer is oviparous, depositing 12 to 24 eggs, usually under flat stones on sunny banks of lakes, rivers, or ponds, or laid in soft, moist soil in fields and forested areas. Hatchlings may be gray on the forward part of the body, with dark brown saddles on the back. There are usually numerous brick-red spots on the edges and center of the ventral scales. However, by the time the snake has grown to a length of about 30 inches, all traces of pattern will have disappeared. Adult specimens are experts at climbing low trees and bushes where they spend a lot of time searching for birds and birds' nests, where they feast on eggs and nestlings. They also feed on all kinds of small mammals, snakes, and lizards.

Florida range: All of Florida, from Panhandle to Keys. Around Cape Canaveral, it shares its territory with a subspecies, the blue racer.

Habitat: Includes mostly forested areas, especially along the borders or fence row thickets around open fields. They are often observed crawling around human dwellings in suburban areas.

EVERGLADES RACER (Blue Racer)
Coluber constrictor paludicola

A slender, blue-gray racer of medium size. Body form, teeth, and scalation is very similar to that of the southern black racer, differing in the much lighter dorsal color.

Coloration: Bluish gray to olive above and, rarely, tan. Belly is white, yellowish or bluish-white. Eyes most frequently red, sometimes amber or yellow. Adults reach an average length of about 45 inches.

The diet of this snake includes rodents, small birds, lizards, snakes, frogs, and insects. When large prey is captured, a loop of the snake's body is thrown over the struggling victim, to hold it down as the snake begins the swallowing process.

Like all racers, the Everglades species is oviparous, and like all, the eggs are coated with small nodules that resemble hard dry grains of salt. Hatchlings are very different in coloration from that of the parents. They are, in early life, usually adorned with 42 to 65 reddish brown dorsal saddles alternating with reddish rounded lateral spots and pinkish belly that may be with or without scattered spots.

Florida range: Found in two discontinuously placed populations. The area around Cape Canaveral in Brevard County is home to this snake, as is the Everglades area from Hendry County eastward to Central Palm Beach County, and westward to Cape Sable.

Habitat: All kinds – fields and forested land, but most frequently observed in limestone flatwoods.

BROWN-CHINNED RACER
Coluber constrictor helvigularis

When in motion and observed from above, this snake may easily be mistaken for the southern black snake. However, except for the chin and lips which may be light tan, brown or mottled, or suffused with these colors, both the dorsal and ventral areas are a uniform black; scales are smooth. All habits are identical to the southern and Everglades species.

Florida range: Found in the Lower Chipola and Apalachicola river valleys and the entire Panhandle.

INDIGO SNAKE – Genus *Drymarchon*

Northern visitors to Florida may recognize here some of the same snakes they encountered back home "in the north". The indigo snake is not among them. This creature likes only a tropical or semi-tropical environment.

Two subspecies are found in the United States. One subspecies occurs throughout Florida and into the southern parts of adjacent gulf states. Another subspecies inhabits Texas, its range extending into Mexico. Wherever the indigo snake occurs in the United States, *it is protected by state and federal law* and appears on the nation's list of endangered animals. It may not be killed, molested nor kept captive.

EASTERN INDIGO SNAKE
Drymarchon corais couperi

A large, rather thick bodied, smooth scaled, blue-black snake; 17 rows of glossy scales, and single anal plate.

The indigo snake attains a length of well over eight feet. It is one of the largest of all North American snakes. Average length is about five feet.

Coloration: Entire upper and undersurfaces (with the exception of the chin and sides of the head) are lustrous black, or blue-black. The chin, throat and upper lip plates are reddish-brown. Specimens having recently shed their skins show all the prismatic colors on the ventral scales.

Although the indigo snake was once classified among the snakes called racers, it lacks the speed of the true racer group. However, it is agile and powerful. Usually a good natured snake when handled carefully. (As an endangered animal, any handling is verboten.) In the wild, when its escape is prevented by an intruder it will assume a very threatening attitude. Flattening its head, it compresses its neck for some inches, so that the latter is flattened vertically. It then arches the neck slightly, and in this eccentric attitude will strike angrily at any nearby object. At the same time, the snake rapidly vibrates its tail.

In spite of the strength indicated by the stout, though graceful, body, the indigo snake is not a constrictor. It feeds in the same manner as do many other snakes, that is, by holding the prey to the ground under a portion of the body and swallowing it at the same time.

Unlike most snakes, which usually confine their food preference either to warm-blooded animals or to cold-blooded animals (amphibians and other reptiles), the indigo snake feeds with equal voracity upon small mammals, birds, frogs, toads, lizards, and other snakes, including poisonous species.

The indigo snake is oviparous; its eggs are about the size of small chicken eggs.

Florida range: Includes the entire state. In the north and central part of the state it inhabits high pine land, and in the south it lives in dry glade areas, tropical hammocks, muckland fields, and some flatwood areas.

WHIPSNAKES – Genus *Masticophis*

Four species of very long-bodied reptiles known as whipsnakes are found in various parts of the southern and western United States. One of the things they have in common is their totally undeserved reputation for attacking people with their whiplike tails. Tall tales claiming that people were whipped to death by one of these snakes, have been handed down from generation to generation. Of course there is not a word of truth in such stories.

One member of the whipsnake clan, the coachwhip, is a Florida resident; it is not however, confined to Florida.

EASTERN COACHWHIP
Masticophis flagellum flagellum

A long, slender, whiplike, and very fast moving snake with a two-tone body.

The eastern coachwhip is one of the largest of the North American snakes.

Coloration: Forward dorsal part of the body is usually black, sometimes brown, becoming paler on the latter half. The tail is pale brown. Ventral scales display clouded edges on the area of the throat; posterior ventral portion is immaculate white or yellowish. However, there are variations within species, with some specimens being sooty-black for about two-thirds their length, then becoming brownish or dark gray toward the tail. The latter coloration is a common occurrence in northern Florida. South Florida specimens are usually pale brown on the head and neck, and pale greenish gray for the greater length of their body.

Scales are smooth. However, the scalation of the

30

long slender tail suggests a braided whip, hence the common names coachwhip and whipsnake. Anal plate is divided.

All whipsnakes are very active, fast moving snakes that usually crawl with the head high above the ground. Escape from danger is this snake's first choice for survival. However, when danger threatens, and the coachwhip can't escape, it is a savage fighter, capable of delivering accurate strikes. These strikes result in deep skin lacerations that bleed profusely.

The average length of an adult specimen is about six feet. Maximum length is over eight feet.

The whipsnake is oviparous, laying from 10 to 24 eggs. Hatchlings usually display a variable number of distinct, narrow, dark crossbands which are separated by narrower light-colored bands.

Diet of an adult specimen includes rodents, birds, lizards and snakes. It will often crawl high in the treetops in search of nesting birds and their eggs.

Florida range: Throughout the state, except for the Keys.

Habitat: Most often observed in high pine-turkey oak; but can be found in almost all open country with well drained soil. Most often found in those areas where there are gopher tortoise burrows – the snake's favorite retreat.

RINGNECK SNAKES – Genus *Diadophis*

All ringneck snakes, of which there are four species, are characteristic in their peculiar coloration – a bright yellow ring about the neck in bold contrast the somber body color of either uniform dark brown or gray. All ringnecks are small slender snakes that average between 10 to 14 inches in length. The scales, smooth and glossy.

Whenever an attempt is made to separate assorted species of ringnecks, it is almost impossible to do so without counting the rows of dorsal scales, and the ventral plates. However, locality alone will in many instances determine the species.

SOUTHERN RINGNECK SNAKE
Diadophis punctatus punctatus

A small, slender, black snake with a slightly flat head and a yellow neck ring; reaches an average length of about 12 inches.

Coloration: Dorsal area is a uniform dark gray to black, except for a yellow neck ring. Ventral parts are yellow to orange with a row of large semicircular, black half-moon shaped spots down the center.

Like all ringneck snakes they are secretive in habit, taking shelter under the loose, rotting bark of fallen trees, among loose rocks or under flat stones and debris of all descriptions; they are rarely observed on the open ground during the daylight hours.

The southern ringneck snake feeds largely upon earthworms and small salamanders, as well as small snakes and lizards.

Although oviparous in classification and it does reproduce by laying eggs, some biologists find it very interesting that the eggs of the species are almost ovoviviparous in view of the fact that the eggs contain large embryos when deposited, and hatch in half the time required for the development of most snakes.

After deposit, eggs increase in size rapidly, and take on irregular shapes. When first deposited, eggs are greatly elongated (about 1¼ inches in length). But at the time of hatching they are about 1½ inches in length, and have assumed peculiar outlines; sometimes they are greatly curved, much like a banana.

Florida range: Distributed throughout the entire state.

Habitat: Usually frequents moist environments, often close to water, under logs, bark, and in the less waterlogged sphagnum beds.

KEY RINGNECK SNAKE
Diadophis punctatus acricus

In this species the head is pale grayish brown, and the chin and lip plates (labials) are only slightly spotted, and the snake is virtually without a neck ring.

This ringneck has the same habitats as the southern ringneck.

Florida range: Confined to Big Pine Key.

Habitat: Lives among pine and scrub vegetation.

RAT SNAKES – Genus *Elaphe*

All members of this group of snakes are large and powerful constrictors, and most are attractive in both coloration and pattern. Members of the genus *Elaphe* may generally be recognized by their flattened bellies; the crawling surface forms almost a right angle with the sides of the body. As Roger Conant, Ph.D., an expert in the field of herpetology, describes them, "In cross sections they are shaped like a loaf of bread" (see illustration).

Mid dorsal scales may be weakly keeled to smooth; anal plate is divided.

The food of rat snakes consists almost entirely of rodents, birds and bird eggs. Most will ascend tall bushes and trees when foraging for birds and their eggs.

Rat snakes are oviparous, and hatchlings are bold in pattern; some may retain the pattern throughout life, while in others the pattern will disappear before they reach maturity. Hatchlings usually are born either with only slightly developed keeled scales on the dorsal side of the body, or they may be born with entirely smooth scales. Young rat snakes may eat lizards and frogs.

All rat snakes have the habit of hissing and vibrating their tails. When disturbed, most will hold their ground against an intruder. Usually the forward part of the body rears upward, the head and neck drawn back in an S-curve, and the mouth held open ready to strike and bite. Often they will hiss as they strike. The teeth, many and sharp, are capable of inflicting many skin punctures or lacerations that should be treated with a good antiseptic.

CORN SNAKE (Red Rat Snake)
Elaphe guttata guttata

A medium sized snake adorned with a bright colored pattern; body moderately stout, proportionately small head, and the scales faintly keeled to smooth.

Distinguishing marks include 40 red, black-edged dorsal blotches, a spear-shaped blotch between the eyes, a black and white checkered belly, two rows of smaller spots along each side, the slightly keeled or unkeeled lower lateral scales, and the divided anal plate. This snake is one of the most strikingly patterned of all North American snakes.

Average length of a Florida corn snake is about three feet.

Coloration: Ground color is reddish brown to grayish or pale red. On the dorsal area is a series of 37 to 48 large blotches narrowly bordered with black; on some specimens a narrow white margin outside the black is present; on each side of the body is a smaller series of similar blotches, and beneath these is a yet smaller series which terminates at the edges of the ventral scales; these lower, smallest spots are more orange than red. In bold contrast to the markings of the sides and dorsal areas, the undersides are white with large black squares.

On the neck and immediately behind the head is a red blotch extending forward in two branches to the top of the head, and then forward to form a wedge or spear shaped marking that ends between the eyes. There is a very pronounced red stripe around the forehead; from behind each eye is a line of similar color, bordered with black, which terminates at the angle of the mouth. The upper and lower lip plates (labials) are whitish with black borders.

Like all rat snakes, the corn snake is an agile climber and will often ascend small trees in search of birds and their eggs. It is also a notorious "ratter", feeding largely on mice and rats of the fields and forests, and is therefore a snake of economic importance to all landowners.

A very active snake which, when surprised, does not ordinarily try to escape, but will instead partially coil, and strike out viciously, and hiss sharply with each strike. It is capable of delivering skin-lacerating bites.

It is oviparous in reproduction, depositing one to dozen yellowish-white eggs that usually hatch in about six to eight weeks. Hatchlings usually have much darker blotches of rich reddish brown; patches of orange between blotches may be present along the mid-dorsal line. A dark bordered stripe extends from the eyes and continues past the mouth to the neck.

ROSY RAT SNAKE
Elaphe guttata rosacea

This pinkish blotched snake is often mistaken for the corn snake, to which it is very similar. The difference is in the rosy rat snake's less intense dorsal pattern; the ventral surface is often plain yellow.

Coloration: The ground color is a cream to buff – a much lighter colored snake than the corn snake; the spots are pink to reddish with the lateral series often nearly absent. The ventral parts may vary from yellow to orange, and although marked anteriorly with some of the faint checkering of the corn snake, posteriorly the checkered pattern is absent. It is a species that is restricted to Florida.

Average length about three and one half feet.

All habits of the rosy rat snake are like those of the corn snake.

Florida range: Southernmost Florida, including the Keys.

Habitat: Hammocks, cultivated areas, edge of wooded areas, groves, and human dwellings.

YELLOW RAT SNAKE
Elaphe obsoleta quadrivittata

A slender snake with stripes and slightly keeled scales. Average length is about 48 inches. Coloration includes a ground color of pale yellow to olive yellow, or pale yellowish brown, with four dark brown stripes extending the length of the body, two on the back and one on each side. The stripes may be rather indistinct on some specimens and very prominent on others. The underparts are pale yellow. Head is paler than the upper body color, and is without stripes. Tongue is black.

The yellow rat snake prefers woodlands and brush covered fields. It is an excellent climber, nearly always ascending the branches of brush or trees to rest or to digest a meal. In fact, it is among the branches of trees and bushes that they are most frequently observed. It commonly invades barns and old deserted buildings in search of rats and mice, or enters chicken coops for the same purpose. In these locations the yellow rat snake can often be found resting in a coiled position, among the rafters. Food consists of warm-blooded prey. Rats and mice and other small mammals probably make up the bulk of its diet. However, small barnyard fowl and their eggs are not rejected when the opportunity arises; the yellow rat snake has a great fondness for bird eggs. With its superb ability to climb, this reptile takes a heavy toll of bird life during the nesting season. Young birds, rats and mice, as well as small eggs are simply swallowed, but larger prey is constricted before being swallowed.

While the yellow rat snake can be very aggressive, if there is any way to escape it will usually retreat in an unhurried manner. However, if challenged, it will put up a bold and courageous fight. The head and neck will be raised well off the ground as the snake faces the intruder, the tail will vibrate rapidly,

37

and when approached too closely, the snake will strike viciously and repeatedly until it can either escape or be subdued.

The yellow rat snake lays about two dozen eggs during late June and early July. They are usually deposited under a fallen decayed tree, rotted stump, or vegetative debris. Hatchlings are about 12 inches long, and are marked quite differently from their parents. They are a dull gray in color, with a series of darker gray or brown blotches on the back. At the age of one year the yellow background color will appear, and the characteristic four-lined pattern will become obvious. From this time on, until they are about two and a half years old, they will reveal the patterns of both immature and mature specimens. The snake matures at the age of three years.

Florida range: Peninsula Florida, possibly extending westward to Madison County in the north, and ranging southward to Lake Okeechobee except for the Levy County territory occupied by the Gulf Hammock species where it is gradually replaced by the Everglades species.

Habitat: A widely distributed species inhabiting open woodlands; common in and around farm buildings, and human dwellings of suburban areas.

GRAY RAT SNAKE
Elaphe obsoleta spiloides

A medium sized, blotched, grayish or whitish snake attaining lengths of 42 to 72 inches, record 84 inches.

Coloration: Pale gray, with a series of large, dark brown saddles along the dorsal area; on the neck these blotches are long and send out narrow extensions from their corners, creating an H-shaped formation. On each side of the body is a series of smaller blotches, and beneath this another, still smaller series at the edges of the ventral plates.

On the back and the sides, a number of scales display white edges when the skin is distended (expanded). The head is gray, dotted with black. There is often a dark band in front of the eyes and usually a wide band from behind each eye to the angle of the mouth. Labials are white, bordered with black. The eyes are silvery.

The forward portion of the undersides is white, irregularly blotched and peppered with gray, and the latter portion is a uniform dark gray. The pattern and coloration just described is usually retained from birth, though its contrast gradually diminishes throughout the snake's life span. Scales are weakly keeled, and the anal plate is divided.

Habits and diet are like those of the other rat snakes.

Florida range: The Panhandle, eastward to Leon County and Union County.

Habitat: Open woodlands and fields.

EVERGLADES RAT SNAKE
Elaphe obsoleta rossalleni

A bright orange colored snake with an average length of 48 inches. A snake that is very similar to the yellow rat snake in both scale characteristics and body form and in having four longitudinal stripes. However, the Everglades species is easily distinguished by color; it has a red tongue, and ventral parts, including the throat, are orange. The longitudinal stripes are less pronounced, sometimes so light as to be hardly perceptible. The scales are weakly keeled; anal plate is divided. This species is restricted to Florida.

Coloration of hatchlings: Background color is pinkish buff or orange; blotches light grayish brown, and not in great contrast to the background color.

Habits: Same as other Florida rat snakes.

Florida range: Northern Dade and Monroe

Counties northward to Palm Beach, Glades and Charlotte Counties. An occasional specimen is encountered in Sarasota and Martin Counties.

Habitat: Swampy wooded areas, glade land, prairies, salt marshes. In the Everglades this snake often leads a semi-arboreal life, living in trees or shrubs along the waterways where it will not hesitate to enter the water if necessary to escape.

GULF HAMMOCK RAT SNAKE
Elaphe obsoleta williamsi

This snake, except for two longitudinal stripes connecting the series of dorsal and lateral blotches, closely resembles the gray rat snake. They are indeed relatives, for the gulf hammock is scientifically classed as a subspecies of the gray rat snake; but unlike its cousin, the gulf hammock rat snake is confined to a small part of Florida.

Florida range: Mainly in the Gulf region of Levy county.

Habitat: Wooded areas in general. Partly arboreal (living above the ground in bushes and trees).

KINGSNAKES – Genus *Lampropeltis*

The many species that make up the genus Lampropeltis are smooth-scaled constricting snakes of small,
medium, and large size. Their popular name is derived
from their habit of killing and consuming both poisonous
and nonpoisonous snakes. They are among the most interesting of the North American snakes. They range in
size from about 14 inches to more than six feet in length.
All are of moderately stout proportions, and all possess
smooth scales – highly polished in most – and proportionately, a rather small head which is hardly distinct from
the neck. The coloration is arranged in transverse bands
or rings and is of striking hues.

Although all of the kingsnakes are powerful constrictors and feed largely on small rodents, they display a
marked inclination toward cannibalism and prey on
snakes other than their own species. This includes all
kinds of poisonous snakes. In their struggle with the latter they are often bitten, but appear to be somewhat immune to the action of snake venom.

To the agriculturist, the kingsnakes are of considerable importance. Their strong, cylindrical bodies, designed for semi-underground existence, enable them to
work their way into burrows of injurious creatures of the
fields as they search for food. Furthermore, they destroy
both the young and the adults of poisonous snakes. However the kingsnakes are not, as it is generally alleged, the
sworn enemies of the dangerous snakes; they are quite as
relentless in constricting and consuming a harmless
species as a poisonous one.

SCARLET KINGSNAKE
Lampropeltis triangulum elapsoides

A small, attractive snake with smooth scales and
adorned with bright yellow, red and black rings.

This little snake represents the greatest development of the ringed pattern; not only do the black rings completely encircle the body, but so do the red and yellow ones.

The scarlet kingsnake is the smallest of the group, as well as the most slender in proportion, and possesses the most pointed snout.

Coloration: This snake is brilliantly ringed with scarlet, yellow, and black. The scarlet rings are the widest and completely encircle the body in the majority of specimens; the yellow rings are about half the width of the scarlet ones and are bordered on each side by rings of black which, on the back, are of about the same width as the yellow. On the sides, the black rings become narrowed (owing to the widening of the yellow) and are very narrow or sometimes broken into blotches on the belly. On the belly, some of the yellow rings enclose spots. There is a yellow ring around the neck immediately behind the head; in front of this is a patch or band of black confined to the top of the head; the pointed snout is red. This red snout distinguishes it from the poisonous coral snake, which has a black nose. There are, of course, other distinguishing marks.

This little kingsnake is found most commonly under loose bark of fallen trees in shady, well watered timber regions.

It is a nocturnal hunter that feeds mostly on salamanders, lizards and small snakes. However, when these are not available, it will not hesitate to feed on nestling birds and small mice. It is a very aggressive snake when capturing prey, but very docile while being handled.

The scarlet kingsnake is oviparous in reproduction; newly hatched young have whitish rings in place of yellow. Otherwise the pattern is like that of the parents.

Florida range: Found throughout the entire state.

MOLE KINGSNAKE
Lampropeltis calligaster rhombomaculata

A smooth, brown, darkly blotched snake. A relatively small, stocky snake with a small head that is almost indistinguishable from the neck. Scales are smooth and glossy, and the snake may be with or without a pattern. In most specimens, the back and tail are covered with a single row of well separated brown blotches that are irregular in form and edged with a narrow border of black. There are smaller, less pronounced spots on the sides. The background color is a lighter brown, becoming yellowish on the lower sides. Underparts are white, checked or spotted with brown. On some, the entire ventral area may be clouded with brown, or covered with pale pinkish red blotches. In some old adults the pattern may be entirely lost, resulting in a "brown" kingsnake, a name once given to these individuals. It is during this period in the snake's life that dusky, lengthwise stripes may appear.

A very secretive, burrowing snake that often surfaces after heavy rain. During dry seasons it remains underground in loose soil, or burrows under rocks or rotted tree stumps. Occasionally specimens are found under stones or logs, but most are found deeper during excavations. Lizards and snakes, as well as salamanders and rodents, are constricted and consumed by this snake. Oviparous in reproduction. Hatchlings are strongly marked with well separated brown or red spots; two lengthwise dark streaks on neck are present. Length of newborns is 8 to 9 inches.

Florida range: Florida Panhandle, eastward to Nassau County and south to central Florida counties from Hernando eastward to northern Brevard County.

43

EASTERN KINGSNAKE
Lampropeltis getulus getulus

This species, the largest of the kingsnakes, is found throughout the eastern United States. The largest specimen recorded measured 82 inches. The body is stout and cylindrical, the head small and barely distinguishable from the neck.

Coloration: The greater number of specimens are black, with narrow yellow or white crossbands which fork on the sides and connect with one another in chainlike fashion. These bands are only one and a half to two scales wide and are separated by intervals of from five to ten scales. The ventral parts are black with large blotches of white or yellow. Florida specimens are usually brown, olive or green, with less distinct bands. Close examination will reveal each scale to contain a pale center. In the northern part of the state, specimens have yellow markings on a black or deep brown background.

This is a very attractive species. The scales of the back are very glossy and those of the ventral parts glossy and lustrous. On specimens that have recently shed their skins, prismatic colors are reflected on the snake's belly.

As mentioned previously, all kingsnakes are cannibalistic; however, the eastern species seems to be the "king of kings" when it comes to devouring other snakes. In their pugnacity, they do not stick to matched opponents, but will take on much bigger snakes, engaging them in a duel to the death. Even very large snakes are able to make but little resistance when encircled by the powerful, constricting coils of the king.

It is this fighting disposition that has given the kingsnake its popular name. Despite its hostility toward other species of snakes, the kingsnake displays a very mild nature toward human captors.

From the standpoint of economic value, this kingsnake performs beneficial work for the agriculturist by destroying rodents, which are injurious to grain crops. Other foods of the kingsnake include birds and their eggs.

Oviparous in reproduction, the eastern kingsnake will deposit 10 to 24 eggs which require from five to six weeks to complete incubation. Hatchlings closely mimic the pattern of the parents.

FLORIDA KINGSNAKE
Lampropeltis getulus floridana

A moderate-sized snake that is speckled and obscurely crossbanded. Average length is about 40 inches.

Coloration: The Florida kingsnake is considered to be the palest in coloration of any of the large kingsnake species and has a chainlike pattern very similar to the eastern species; however, the Florida species has more crossbands (46 to 85, average 66) and the bands do not fork on the sides. There is a lateral series of light vertical spots alternating with the crossbands. The ground color is dark brown or blackish, but each scale has a white or yellowish spot which sometimes tends to obscure the banding. Ventral parts are cream to pale yellow with spots of tan or pinkish brown.

Oviparous in reproduction. Young display a more pronounced chainlike pattern, with dorsal crossbands that are cream colored, yellow, or reddish yellow on a ground color of brown; many scales in the dark dorsal areas have reddish brown centers.

Florida range: Central and southern Florida except for the extreme tip of the peninsula.

Habitat: Near cypress ponds, in savannah lands and prairies. This subspecies intergrades with the eastern species in northern and central Florida.

SCARLET and SHORT-TAILED SNAKES
Genera *Cemophora* and *Stilosoma*

Two small snakes sometimes seen in Florida share one characteristic with the several snakes (rat snakes and kingsnakes) described above; they too, are constrictors. Otherwise, they have little in common with the large constrictors – or with each other. In appearance, they are totally different; however, they are constrictors all.

FLORIDA SCARLET SNAKE
Cemophora coccinea

These small snakes have a moderately slender, very cylindrical body with brightly colored cross-bands, and reach an average length of 16 inches.

Coloration: Pattern of red, black, and yellow cross-bands that do not encircle the body completely; ventral parts are white or yellow. The nose is pointed and pinkish red, as is the top of the head before the eyes; scales are smooth. The anal plate is undivided.

When the scarlet snake is viewed from above, the pattern appears as wide crimson or scarlet rings separated by pairs of narrow black ones, the latter enclosing an equal-sized ring of yellow. It is this ringed appearance that causes the species to resemble the coral snake and the scarlet kingsnake; however, the poisonous coral snake has wide scarlet rings, and equal-sized rings of black, and very narrow yellow rings – barely a scale wide – bordering the black. It should be understood that when we speak of rings, we mean that the color completely encircles the body. The scarlet kingsnake also looks very much like the scarlet snake, but the former is *ringed* with the colors. When examined from the side, the scarlet snake may be described as actually having large scarlet *bands* broadly bordered with black, separated by *bands* of yellow. These bands are not truly rings, as they do not continue onto the belly of the snake.

The bright little scarlet snake also resembles the kingsnakes in feeding habits; both include small lizards, snakes and mice in the diet, and subdue their prey by constriction.

The scarlet snake is very secretive, and seems to pass most of its life burrowing its way with the aid of its sharp nose.

It is oviparous, and lays eight to ten white, elongated eggs. Scarlet snakes have been known to swallow their own eggs, displaying a real act of cannibalism. Young specimens have immaculate white bands separating the black bands or partial rings.

Florida range: Found throughout the Florida mainland.

Habitat: Usually found burrowing in leaf mold, decayed logs, moist loam, or muck and peat soil, and under the loose bark of dead trees.

SHORT-TAILED SNAKE
Stilosoma extenuatum

A small, slender snake with a very short tail, which reaches an average length of 14 inches.

Coloration: Silvery gray ground color on the dorsal area with about 60 black-bordered brown blotches from the head to the base of the tail – on which there are a dozen more blotches. Along the dorsal line the blotches are separated by areas of red, yellow or orange. Silvery gray belly area is strongly marked with brown or black blotches which extend upward toward the lighter areas that separate the dark dorsal blotches.

A small constrictor that feeds on small lizards and other snakes, the short-tailed snake is a very secretive, burrowing snake. It is sometimes encountered as it rests or hunts under rocks, rotted stumps, fallen logs, loose bark, and debris. When disturbed, this little snake will vibrate its tail vigorously, and strike at the intruder with a hissing sound. Not very much is known about this rather rare snake's reproductive habits, except that it is oviparous, laying up to a dozen eggs. Hatchlings are exact duplicates of the parents.

Florida range: The central part of the peninsula. Known in Alachua, Marion, Citrus, Lake, Seminole, Orange, Hernando, Pinellas and Polk counties.

Habitat: Longleaf pine areas, turkey oak ridges; upland hammocks.

FLORIDA PINE SNAKE
Pituophis melanoleucus mugitus

This constrictor is the Florida representative of a larger group known throughout much of the United States as bullsnakes.

A large, rusty brown, blotched snake with a bad temper and an awful hiss. Average length five feet.

Coloration: Ground color rusty brown with three series of darker brown blotches, often indistinct, especially on the anterior part of the body.

A very ill-tempered snake that is always ready to strike at anyone who threatens its safety. If there is any opportunity for escape the pine snake will take it, but if escape is denied, this snake will prepare to defend itself. It will face the intruder, raise the forward part of its body until head is high in the air, take a deep breath, and expel it with a loud, prolonged hiss. During this defensive attitude, the tail vibrates rapidly. It is a powerful constrictor that feeds on warm-blooded prey. Rodents, rabbits, birds and their eggs make up the bulk of the diet.

Oviparous in reproduction, it lays six to a dozen eggs. The hatchlings are vividly patterned; across the front of the face of the young snakes is a dark, masklike line, very much like the mask of a raccoon. The dorsal blotches are chestnut brown.

Florida range: known throughout most of Florida, from Escambia County southward to Dade County.

Habitat: High pinelands; sandy areas.

HOGNOSE SNAKES – Genus *Heterodon*

Hognose snakes are very interesting creatures – both in form and behavior.

In proportion to body length, they are rather thick-bodied; all possess a peculiar upturned, shovel-like snout, which of course gave them the name "hognose".

The uninitiated are likely to mistake this strikingly patterned snake for a poisonous species; that suspicion is sure to be enhanced by the bizarre behavior that it exhibits when confronted. First, it will flatten its head and neck to a great degree, and hiss loudly. (In some localities this performance has earned it the name "puff adder" or "sand adder".) In their ability to dilate the neck, the snakes resemble the cobras of the eastern hemisphere, and the action is indeed performed using the same kind of mechanism employed by the cobras. The spreading is accomplished by means of long ribs that lie close along the backbone when the body is in a passive condition, but spread laterally when the snake is excited or angry.

But here the resemblance ends. With its antics the hognose manages to give an impression of ferocity seldom seen among nonpoisonous snakes; yet it is not only nonpoisonous – it can rarely, if ever, be induced to bite.

If the spreading and hissing fails to frighten an intruder away, the hognose snake will continue with its bag of tricks by feigning death. It very convincingly "plays 'possum". The tongue dangles loosely from the side of the wide open mouth and the snake appears to be seized by convulsions as it writhes in apparent agony that ends with a spasmodic wriggling of the tail.

50

Suddenly it turns on its back and lies limp, in all appearances – dead. So patiently does this snake feign death that it may be carried by the tail for a long time without displaying any sign of life. This author once placed a specimen (doing its dead snake act) in his daughter's wading pool where it remained on its back as it floated about on the surface of the water. There are ways, however, to cause the snake to betray itself. One is to leave the scene so that the snake cannot see you. When convinced that you are gone, it will slowly close its mouth, retract its tongue and raise its head, looking about to see if escape is possible. When it feels safe it will turn on its belly and crawl away. The second way, rather comically, is to turn the "dead" reptile on its belly – whereupon it quickly flips belly-up again. It seems, according to this creature's reasoning, that to appear thoroughly dead one should be on one's back! This behavior is consistent and can be repeated over and over.

All this drama is produced only as a last resort. Like most snakes, the hognose's first impulse when danger threatens is to escape.

In the three species of hognose snakes, the dentition (teeth) differs from that of most of the other nonpoisonous snakes of Colubridae, the large family to which they belong. On each side of the posterior portion of the upper jaw is a fanglike tooth. (It is not a true fang, as it is not hollow.) Most other members of the colubrid family that have rear fangs use them to inject poison, but the "fangs" of the hognose snake are entirely free of venom; they are used instead only to hold prey, as these snakes possess no power of bodily constriction.

The primary source of food for the hognose snake is toads, which have a powerful skin poison that can sicken or kill predators. Interestingly, these snakes appear to be immune to it. The protecting substance is believed to be a secretion of the greatly enlarged adrenal glands of the hognose snakes. The two large, fanglike teeth are used to deflate the lungs of toads, which attempt to avoid being swallowed by puffing up their bodies to two or three times normal size. The snake swallows as much as it can of the front part of the toad's body, which puts the toad's lungs in contact with the fangs. One quick puncture, and the toad is reduced to a size then easily swallowed.

EASTERN HOGNOSE SNAKE
Heterodon platyrhinos

A stout-bodied black or blotched snake with an upturned snout which is exaggerated by the upturned, keeled rostral (nose) plate.

Average length of this species is about 28 inches. However, lengths of over a yard are not uncommon; the record is $45\frac{1}{2}$ inches. A 28-inch specimen presented the following measurements:

Total length	28 inches
Length of tail	$4\frac{1}{2}$ inches
Greatest diameter	$1\frac{1}{4}$ inches
Width of head	1 inch
Length of head	$1\frac{3}{8}$ inches
Height of rostral plate	$\frac{1}{4}$ inch

There are 25 rows of scales, keeled except for the lower two or three rows, which may be either smooth or weakly keeled; 123 to 148 ventral plates are present, subcaudal plates (underside of tail) number 39 to 56.

Rostral (nose) plate is upturned with a transverse keel.

Labial (lip) plates: upper, eight plates, lower labials, 11. Anal plate, divided.

Coloration: Background color is gray, yellow or sometimes reddish. Patterns vary, but all are intricate, usually having a main series of 28 quadrate (square or rectangular) dorsal blotches and one, sometimes several, series of smaller lateral blotches. However, some specimens are almost solid black. Belly is greenish yellow with faint dark blotches. Some may have solid black bellies; underside of tail is usually lighter than the belly color. Some specimens may display a tint of bright brick red on the top of the neck. Head is most often brown to yellowish brown, with a dark band crossing the top, just in front of the eyes. Usually, behind the eyes is a broken band which branches out to form other bands and extends into the area of the neck to form two large blotches. A short band extends from the eye to the angle of the mouth.

The eastern hognose snake prefers high pine country and upland hammocks throughout the entire state, except for the Keys.

Hognose snakes are oviparous, laying about 24 eggs. The shell is leathery and covered with a sort of mucous that causes the eggs to stick together. Eggs are left to hatch by the heat of the sun. Except for being much brighter, the hatchlings are exact duplicates of the parents. Average length of a newborn is about eight inches.

SOUTHERN HOGNOSE SNAKE
Heterodon simus

Considerably smaller and stouter in form than the eastern species, this snake attains a length of about 20 inches. The shovel-like rostral plate is more prominent and very sharply upturned.

Coloration: Pale brownish gray above, with a series of large, rather irregular patches of blackish brown on the back; between these blotches the body color is slightly paler than on the sides. Below these spots, on each side of the snake, is a row of smaller spots, alternating with those above. With the exception of this smaller row of spots on the sides, the ground color presents a plain, unspotted surface; the belly also lacks spots. This is in great contrast to the eastern (and more widely distributed) species in which both the sides of the reptile and the belly plate are profusely spotted or blotched with black.

At a glance, the pattern of the southern species appears plainer and less sharply defined than that of the eastern species, but the arrangement of the bolder markings is very similar. There is a broken band across the top of the head, and another band from the eye to the angle of the mouth. On the back of the neck (nape) are two large blotches. Variations occur among individuals; the body varies from gray to yellow, with many specimens having a tinge of brick-red on the neck or over a considerable part of the anterior portion of the body.

Habits of this snake, including reproduction, are like those of the eastern species. However, habitats are somewhat different. Though sometimes encountered in upland hammocks, the southern species seems to prefer dry floodplains of rivers, wire grass flatwoods, fields and groves. And in feeding, while this species has no objection to occasionally adding frogs to its diet, it seems to like toads most of the time.

Florida range: Includes all of the northern portion of the state, southward into the peninsula as far as Pinellas County.

GREEN SNAKES – Genus *Opheodrys*

Two species of small, pale green snakes inhabit North America, where both are widely distributed. Because of their uniform color (both lack any trace of markings), they are quite distinct and may be immediately recognized as *Opheodrys*. It may appear more difficult to separate the two species, as one precisely matches the other in coloration of the dorsal area. It is only by the scalation that they may be differentiated. Florida snake watchers need not worry about misidentification, for Florida is inhabited by only one species of the genus, the rough green snake.

ROUGH GREEN SNAKE
Opheodrys aestivus

A very slender, green snake, having a very long and gradually tapering tail, and distinctly keeled scales.

Coloration: Uniform bright leaf green above, ventral areas bright yellow; average length about 28 inches.

The rough green snake is a climbing species, frequenting bushes and low trees. It is insectivorous, feeding on all kinds of soft-bodied insects. When climbing among the green leaves and branches, its harmonizing shade matches the foliage so perfectly that the snake is almost impossible to see. This snake is capable of traveling among the branches more quickly than the human eye can follow.

Oviparous in reproduction, the female lays four to twelve very elongated eggs under a flat stone, usually at the edge of a grassy field and near a treeline. Eggs usually are found adhered to one another in pairs. Hatchlings are grayish green to pale, delicate green.

Florida range: Northern Florida southward as far as Dade County.

Habitat: Upland hammocks; high pine and flat woods, in bushes and trees.

GARTER and RIBBON SNAKES –
Genus *Thamnophis*

The various species of this genus are characterized by their pattern – usually three narrow yellow stripes upon a darker ground color. One of the stripes is on the back; the others are on the lower portion of the sides.

The striped snakes are the most abundant of North American snakes. They inhabit every part of the continent in which snakes are found and extend as far southward as Central America. From a structural standpoint, they are closely related to the water snakes, a relationship also demonstrated by the semi-aquatic habits of some of the species. All of the species produce living young, generally in great numbers, which explains the general abundance of these reptiles.

This group of striped snakes feeds entirely upon cold-blooded creatures: frogs, toads, fishes, and worms. All of the species are quite harmless and inoffensive.

EASTERN GARTER SNAKE
Thamnophis sirtalis sirtalis

A medium-sized snake, olive to brownish in color with three distinct longitudinal yellowish stripes; average length, 18 inches.

This snake displays many variations in color and some variation in details of the spotting and checkerboard pattern to be seen on the dorsal surface between the distinct stripes. One stripe runs down the middle of the back and one along each side on the second and third row of scales. Ventral parts are greenish white to yellowish, with narrow black edging near the ends of the ventral plates.

Head is the same color as the dorsal ground color; labial plates are the same color as the ventral parts – greenish or yellowish. Just described is the most common combination of color and pattern. Stripes on some individuals may be brownish, greenish or bluish. Some specimens may even lack stripes entirely. Sometimes the spots or checkering may be more prominent than the stripes or vice versa.

Although this species seems to favor moist locations, it may be observed in all kinds of habitats within its range. It is a snake that may be encountered anywhere: forests, open fields, backyard gardens, roadsides, vacant lots, parks, close to bodies of water, as well as among all types of debris, including tires, wooden boards, pieces of cardboard, newspapers, flat stones, and even in discarded tin cans.

The food of this garter snake consists mainly of earthworms, frogs, toads, tadpoles, crayfish, salamanders, assorted insects, and when possible, an occasional fish. Only on rare occasions will it feed on warm blooded prey – hatchling birds and nesting small mammals. When first encountered, if escape seems impossible, it becomes very aggressive and will strike relentlessly at the object of intrusion. Large specimens are capable of inflicting many bleeding skin lacerations. Garter snakes are particularly noted for the scent from musk glands which are located at the underbase of the tail, the anus. When irritated, the snake is prone to discharge the strong, foul-smelling secretion.

This garter snake, like all others, is ovoviviparous in reproduction and newborns are exact duplicates of their parents, except that they are much brighter in coloration and pattern.

Florida range: Found throughout the entire state, including the panhandle and many of the upper Keys.

Habitat: While this species favors open, moist areas, it is found in practically every type of environment within its range.

EARTH SNAKES – Genus *Virginia*

There are two distinct species of earth snakes that are native to Florida. Both are without distinctive markings. These 7- to 10-inch long snakes must be closely examined for accurate identification to make sure of the species at hand. Any small snake, hatchling or adult, with comparable colors can easily be mistaken for an earth snake.

EASTERN or SMOOTH EARTH SNAKE
Virginia valeriae

A tiny brown snake that has a record length of $13\frac{1}{4}$ inches, but averages about 7 to 10 inches in length. Head is narrow; body moderately stout; tail is short and abruptly tapered. Coloration includes a grayish to reddish brown background color, usually without markings. In some specimens the background color may be adorned with four longitudinal rows of black dots that may appear to be lines; belly is whitish. Most scales are smooth; those on the posterior portion of the body may be keeled. Close examination must be made of the keeled scales, as some specimens may have faint, light colored thin lines on them which may present a false keeled appearance.

This is a snake of secretive habits, usually preferring leaf mold coverage, as they hide under rocks, decayed logs and forest and field debris.

Food includes earthworms and soft bodied insects and their larvae. Earth snakes produce live offspring and usually give birth to seven to eight young which are no thicker than an ordinary wooden match. The body of an adult specimen measuring about seven inches in length will have a body diameter of a quarter of an inch.

Florida range: Northern Florida, southward to Alachua county.

ROUGH EARTH SNAKE
Virginia striatula

A very small snake with a narrow head. In this species the scales are all keeled and are in 17 rows. Average length is 7 to 10 inches, record $12^3/_4$ inches. Coloration: Plain gray or brown above, sometimes with a vague light band across the back of the head; belly yellowish to pink. Anal plate usually divided.

The rough ground snake differs from the smooth species in that the smooth species has 15 rows of smooth scales with a few keeled scales at the posterior part of the body, while in the rough species the scales are all keeled and in 17 rows. Florida range is the same as that of the smooth species. Habitats include acid flatwoods, under logs about cypress ponds and bayheads.

EASTERN WORM SNAKE
Carphophis amoenus amoenus

A small, brown colored snake with a moderately stout body and a short, abruptly tapering tail which terminates into a sharp point. Head not distinct from the neck. Its 13 rows of smooth scales are very glossy, as are the ventral plates which average about 118 plates among the males, and about 124 among the females. Belly is bright pink in color. Tail is very short, accounting for about one-sixth or less of the snake's total length, which rarely exceeds 12 inches; average length is usually less than 10 inches.

This small snake leads a secretive life, and is rarely observed in open areas. Preferred habitat is forested areas where it is often discovered under stones, logs, rotting leaves, and other forest debris. It has been found under the bark of decayed logs.

Food consists of all kinds of small worms and soft bodied larvae of insects that burrow into decaying logs or live under damp debris of the forest floor.

The worm snake, oviparous in reproduction, lays small elongated, soft, leathery-shelled eggs. Newly hatched young are darker in color than the parents, and measure about $3\frac{1}{2}$ inches in length, $\frac{1}{8}$ inch in diameter. During their early days they will be found in small anthills in search of the larvae.

Florida range: Northern Florida southward to Pinellas County.

Habitat: Usually found under stones, or logs, or in rotting wood in moist forested areas.

WATER SNAKES

No state is more generously endowed with wet environments than Florida. Not only do we have numerous rivers, lakes, ponds, canals, drainage ditches, and swamps, we have the longest coastline of any continental state, with myriad bays and inlets. It should be no surprise then, that there are among the serpent population many members that, like humans, enjoy basking and "water sports"!

While there are several species that are generally called "water snakes", there are many others that have an affinity for (and make their homes in) the huge expanse of swamp, salt marsh, and other watery areas.

Many of the water snakes belong to the genus *Nerodia*.

BANDED WATER SNAKE
Nerodia fasciata fasciata

This heavy-bodied, dark snake has crossbands along the entire length of the body, and averages three feet in length.

Coloration: The entire length of the body is marked with brown crossbands; broad on the back, they become narrower on the sides. Bands may vary in number from 19 to 33. In mature individuals the bands may be obscure, the back appearing a uniform brown to black. However, the lower sides will have triangular areas (of the lighter ground color) which formerly separated the bands. The ventral parts are yellowish and marked with quadrate reddish spots. The head is rather flat, and quite distinct from the neck. The head markings are fairly constant; the top of the head is dark in color and there is a dark band that runs from behind the eye to the angle of the jaw. Lip plates are yellow with dark borders. The top of the head is covered with smooth, glossy plates that sharply contrast with the dull surface of the dorsal area. Old specimens are almost uniformly brown or black on the upper parts, but the brilliant red spots are always present on the ventral parts.

The banded water snake inhabits swamps and marshlands, and borders of quiet lakes, ponds, rivers, and drainage ditches.

Frogs and fish are the main foods of this snake, which forages mostly during the night. However, it very seldom strays far from the water, its preferred avenue of escape. When first encountered it will strike viciously, and is capable of inflicting a serious wound with its sharp, slightly curved teeth. Such a wound should always be immediately treated with a good antiseptic. The snake is most often encountered on the shoreline, or among the low branches of trees and shrubs that overhang the water. Like all water snakes this species, when disturbed, will give off an offensive odor, produced by the secretion contained in the musk glands located just under the anal plate. Captive specimens, more often than not, become adjusted to being handled and will breed regularly when given clean, even-temperatured housing.

Ovoviviparous in reproduction. Young have a bright pattern that begins to fade during their second summer. They will bite, and their musk glands are well developed at birth.

Florida range: The entire Panhandle, east to Baker County in the north, and southwest to Levy and Marion counties.

Habitat: Aquatic environments, preferably small marshes and bodies of water rather than the larger rivers and lakes.

FLORIDA WATER SNAKE
Nerodia fasciata pictiventris

This subspecies is identical in habit and habitat to the banded water snake, but its appearance and range differ slightly. Its ventral markings have red and black blotches which encircle pale, oval spots, making the belly appear to have wavy lines across it.

Florida range: All of peninsular Florida.

BROWN WATER SNAKE
Nerodia taxispilota

A heavy bodied, rough scaled, blotched, brown snake with an average length of three and one half feet.

Coloration: Ground color is reddish brown. There is a mid-dorsal row of 25 squarish, blackish blotches, and below that on each side is a row of similar but smaller blotches well separated from, and alternating with, those of the mid-dorsal row. Ventral parts are usually yellow, and heavily blotched with brown or black. Because of the subtriangular shape of the head, much like that of the poisonous cottonmouth, it is imperative that you learn proper identification before going into this snake's habitat. The two snakes – brown water snakes and cottonmouths – inhabit the same environment of freshwater lakes, rivers, drainage ditches, swamps and ponds.

This snake seems to enjoy basking more than any other water snake. It is a gregarious creature that can often be observed basking on the same object (rock, log or overhanging tree) with others of its kind. An excellent climber, it often chooses the branches of a bush that overhangs the water for its social get-togethers. Although escape is its first choice, it will, when molested, stand its ground and strike savagely at the intruder. Fish, frogs, toads, salamanders, and even small turtles are eaten by this snake.

Florida range: Northern and central Florida, southward to Lake and Lee counties.

Habitat: Rivers, creeks, alluvial swamps, and lakes.

GREEN WATER SNAKE
Nerodia cyclopion cyclopion

A rough-scaled, heavy bodied, dark greenish to olive snake with a rather obscure pattern, and an average length of three feet. It is believed to be the

65

largest in body and the longest of all nonpoisonous water snakes.

Coloration: The weakly defined dorsal pattern consists of about 50 narrow, dark crossbands that alternate with a lateral series of the same hue, on a ground color of dark to olive green. These markings tend to fade with age. The head is comparatively long, with a puffy appearance, especially the upper lip plates. The pupils are round and placed high and forward on the head. The ventral parts are pale yellow, anteriorly, while the posterior two-thirds is grayish brown and marked with half-moon-shaped semi-circles of white or yellow on each ventral plate.

Inhabits bodies of slow moving fresh water lakes, rivers and swamps.

Despite its bulkiness, this snake is a good climber and can sometimes be observed basking among tree branches that overhang the water. Fields, pine forests, and cypress ponds and swamps are the preferred habitats and on the rare occasions it may be encountered lying on the shoreline, very close to the water. It prefers to stay in the water much of the time because its great bulk puts it at a disadvantage on land, where it is unable to move as fast. In the water, however, it swims rapidly and gracefully. Fish and frogs comprise the majority of its diet, and most foraging for food is done during the night. It is usually ill-tempered, and strikes with speed and accuracy, in spite of its robust structure. The large jaws are armed with sharp, curved teeth that are capable of inflicting a nasty slashing wound, which should be immediately treated with a good antiseptic. Ovoviviparous in reproduction, the green water snake gives birth to 10 to 15 living young which are somewhat brighter in color than their parents.

Florida range: Escambia and Leon counties in the western Panhandle.

Habitat: Lakes, marshes, and rivers, usually in quiet waters.

FLORIDA GREEN WATER SNAKE
Nerodia cyclopion floridana

This snake looks very much like the green water snake, *Nerodia cyclopion cyclopion.* However, this snake's belly is whitish, whereas *N.c.c.* has a yellowish or brownish belly, and the ventral patterns are somewhat different. Some individuals may have small spots along the edges of the ventral scales. Other points of separation are in the scale count – *Nerodia cyclopion floridana* males and females alike usually have 29 scale rows. *Nerodia cyclopion cyclopion* males have 29 rows while the females have 31 rows. Ventral plates average about 137 (132 to 142) in *N.c.f.,* and about 142 (136 to 148) in *N.c.c.* To go even further, *N.c.c.* males have a subcaudal scale count of 68 to 78, females 57 to 70. *N.c.f.* males have 80 to 84, and females 69 to 78. But a point that separates both green species from all the other water snakes is the presence of scales between the eye and lip plates. In all other water snakes, at least one of the lip scales extends all the way up to eye.

Florida range: Northeastern and peninsular Florida, from Leon county eastward and southward.

Habitat: Shorelines of large lakes, marshes, quiet waters generally.

STRIPED CRAYFISH SNAKE
Regina alleni

A small, moderately stout snake with a short tail, small head and indistinct neck, and an average length of about 15 inches. Scales are smooth on the head and trunk, but keeled in the region of the anus and the top of the tail. Anal plate is divided.

Coloration: It has a dorsal pattern of longitudinal stripes that includes a broad, dark brown, mid-dorsal stripe, a pale yellowish or olive stripe below this, another brown stripe under this, and still lower, on the bottom three scale rows, is a yellow or olive stripe. Ventral parts are usually yellowish, but in some specimens, may be orange to orange brown, and may or may not have a few scattered dusky patches. Also, some may have a well defined mid-ventral row of spots running the length of the trunk.

This snake frequents the heavily moist environment of swamps, sloughs and sphagnum bogs and also, lakes and rivers with heavy concentration of water hyacinths.

This crayfish snake is secretive in habit, and is often encountered under logs, and field and forest debris. Dragging or raking water hyacinths up onto the shoreline will usually produce a few specimens. This snake can often be observed crawling on country roads during or soon after a heavy rainfall.

Crayfish seem to be the favorite food of this snake, but salamanders of all descriptions will be devoured, as well as frogs and leeches.

Ovoviviparous in reproduction, the offspring at birth display the same pattern and coloration as their parents.

Florida range: Extreme eastern edge of the panhandle, and southward throughout the entire peninsula.

Habitat: Alluvial swamps, burrowing in the mud.

QUEEN CRAYFISH SNAKE
Regina septemvittata

A slender, brownish, rough scaled, striped snake with an average length of about fifteen inches.

Coloration: The ground color is usually brown, rich, and dark. Young specimens usually have three even darker stripes that run the entire length of the dorsal area. In most adult specimens these stripes are indistinct or lacking entirely. All however, have a 1½-scale wide, yellow stripe along each side on the first and second row of scales. This is bordered below by a chestnut brown band on the lower half of the first row of scales and the edges of the ventral plates. Ventral parts are pale yellow and have rows of gray to brown spots forming two stripes, which join to form a single mid-ventral stripe under the throat, and another, for a short distance in front of the anal plate and under the tail. The upper lip plates and nose scale, are pale yellow.

This snake enjoys small ponds and slow moving rivers where it feeds almost exclusively on crayfish. It has also been observed feeding on frogs, tadpoles, and fish.

The queen crayfish snake can often be seen basking on any flat object close to, or in the water. On the ground it seems to choose a spot near a rock or other object that would afford a quick hiding place or escape from a predator. It will occasionally ascend branches that overhang the water.

Florida range: The Apalachicola drainage, and is known in Jackson and Liberty counties.

Habitat: Borders of rivers and ponds.

PINE WOODS SNAKE
Rhadinaea flavilata

A small, smooth scaled, brown snake with a yellow ventral area, and an average length of about ten inches.

Coloration: Dorsal areas are usually reddish brown to golden brown with a soft iridescence and sometimes with a faint, narrow median dark stripe. There is a dark band that runs from the eye to the corner of the mouth. Ventral parts as well as the lips are yellow with a few black spots on some of the lip plates.

The pine woods snake, once called the "yellow lip snake", is a very secretive snake that prefers heavily wooded areas, where it spends a large part of its time crawling under decayed leaves, stumps, and fallen logs in its search for worms and grubs, as well as a variety of soft bodied insects and their larvae. When at rest, its favorite hiding place is under the loose bark of a decaying tree, or under debris of all descriptions.

Oviparous in reproduction. Hatchlings usually have more pronounced dark, dorsal and side stripes.

Florida range: From northern and central Florida southward to Indian River County.

Habitat: Damp locales in flatwoods and hammocks, under logs, loose bark or other forest debris as well as rubbish near human dwellings. However, flatwoods bordering on cypress swamps and ponds seem to be the first preference of this snake.

MUD and RAINBOW SNAKES –
Genus *Farancia*

These large snakes are aquatic in habit, and are designed to overpower and eat slippery amphibians and slimy eels. They are attractive in pattern and color. Intensifying their brilliant pattern is the opalescent luster of the smooth scales.

Despite their large size, they are burrowing snakes and rarely expose themselves by foraging above ground during daylight hours. However, during heavy daytime rain periods they do move about in open areas.

They are snakes that are at home in the water, and are expert swimmers and divers.

EASTERN MUD SNAKE
Farancia abacura

A large, glossy-scaled, black and red snake with a very short tail.

Coloration: Purplish black above, with large, red, inverted V-shaped blotches on the sides. The underside is a rich red with many black patches. The sides of the head are reddish, with a row of large black spots extending along the upper lip plates.

The average length is about four feet, reaching a maximum length of about six feet.

This burrowing snake is usually found in swampy timber areas, where it takes shelter under fallen and decaying tree trunks.

The eyes are small, dull, poorly developed, and essentially fitted for a subterranean life. However, the snake is quite active and capable of crawling over

71

the ground with considerable speed. It also swims and dives with great agility.

The mud snake is oviparous, laying from 10 to 48 blunt, oval eggs; the eggs are yellowish white with a smooth leathery shell.

Florida range: Except for the extreme western Panhandle, the mud snake is distributed throughout the state.

Habitats: Marshes, swamps, large ponds, drainage ditches, and sloughs.

RAINBOW SNAKE
Farancia erytrogramma

A large, heavy bodied snake with highly glossed scales and a gaudily striped body. Average length is about four feet.

Coloration: A purplish black or rich, deep, dark blue; along the back, from neck to tail, are three stripes of dark red or sometimes deep orange. A band of pale yellow runs along the sides. The underside is red, with two rows of large blue-black spots running the length of the body; between these is a row of much smaller spots, beginning some distance from the neck and extending to within a short distance of the tail. The head is dark, with obscure red markings; upper lip plates are yellow and each plate contains a large, black spot. The anal plate is sometimes divided, sometimes single.

The rainbow snake lives in swampy wooded areas and along banks of slow moving rivers, where it burrows into the damp soil or into and under decayed and fallen trees. It is not considered a hostile snake when caught and handled. However, some specimens have been known to bite, sometimes viciously.

The rainbow snake is oviparous, depositing 24 to 50 bluntly oval, white eggs that have smooth leathery shells. Eggs usually hatch in about two months. Hatchlings measure about nine inches, and display the pattern of the parents.

Young feed on earthworms, small frogs, salamanders, and tadpoles. Adults feed on all kinds of amphibians and fish, especially eels.

Florida range: Northern and north central Florida, southwest to Marion County.

Habitat: Swampy areas and rivers, often underground.

BROWN and REDBELLY SNAKES
Genus *Storeria*

All members of this genus are small, secretive snakes that are most often brown in color but vary to gray or reddish on the dorsal area. Scales are keeled, and the anal plate is divided. These snakes have the habit of flattening their bodies when confronted, very much like many of the water snakes to which they are related. (In fact, some biologists describe these little snakes as being degenerate descendants of the group of water snakes.) They are recognized by the dull brown color of the dorsal area, with only obscure markings or none whatever. Their maximum length is about 14 inches. They are generally familiar to most observers as the little "ground snakes" so often found hiding under flat stones or the loose bark of decaying trees. All are ovoviviparous in reproduction.

FLORIDA BROWN SNAKE
Storeria dekayi victa

A small brownish snake with a more or less spotted back, and an average length of about 14 inches.

Coloration: Ground color brown or tan with a variable amount of spotting of the scales of the sixth row. At the back of the head is a light crossband followed by a dark crossband. Ventral parts are whitish, often with a black spot on the outer end of each ventral plate.

A very secretive snake that usually spends the daylight hours resting under debris of all kinds, rotted logs, and among water hyacinths. It is an expert swimmer, feeding on small aquatic creatures, earthworms, grubs, slugs, and soft bodied beetles and their larvae.

The Florida brown snake is ovoviviparous and gives birth to five to fifteen living young. Newborns are usually much darker in coloration than the parents. The whitish collar is very prominent in the young.

Florida range: From northern Florida southward to Cape Sable. In the panhandle it is replaced by the midland brown snake.

Habitat: Cypress swamp areas, wet prairies, ponds, and drainage ditches, especially those with water hyacinths.

MIDLAND BROWN SNAKE
Storeria dekayi wrightorum

A small, brown snake usually having a pattern of crossbands and an average length of about 10 inches; maximum about 16 inches.

Coloration: Brownish on the dorsal areas with about 75 black crossbands, each being about one-half of a scale wide and extending to about the sixth scale row. Vague lateral spots alternate with the crossbands. Ventral parts are whitish with scattered dark specks on the outer edges of the ventral plates.

During the daylight hours this little brown snake often prefers to hide or rest under all kinds of debris, under loose bark of decaying trees, logs, and stumps. It may also be encountered on roadways during or after heavy rains. Soft bodied insects and their larvae are consumed by this snake, all being hunted from dusk to nightfall.

Gives birth to 4 to 12 living young which are similar to their parents in coloration. Young feed upon slugs, earthworms, and small soft-bodied insects.

Florida range: The Panhandle; Gadsen, Liberty and Escambia counties.

75

Habitat: Frequently found under stones or debris, almost always close to water.

FLORIDA REDBELLY SNAKE
Storeria occipitomaculata obscura

A small black snake with a reddish or pinkish ventral area. Average length about 7 inches.

Coloration: Dorsal area black, with a light neck ring; ventral area may be red or pink, and may or may not display some spotting. Top and sides of head are black. On the fifth lip plate is a light spot that extends downward to the edge of the mouth. Spots on the neck fuse to form a light collar around the neck.

This small snake may be encountered under leaf mold, in garden and flower beds in light loam or plant debris. Food seems to be confined to snails, slugs and earthworms. Ovoviviparous, the young are similar to the parents in pattern; however, coloration is always somewhat darker.

Florida range: Northern Florida southward to Marion County and Charlotte County. Intergrades with the northern redbelly species in the western Panhandle.

Habitat: The woodlands, in leaf mold; home gardens and flower beds, in light loam or debris.

NORTHERN REDBELLY SNAKE
Storeria occipitomaculata occipitomaculata

A small, slender, smooth-scaled snake that intergrades, in the Panhandle, with the Florida redbelly snake. It is a blotched snake with a short tail that measures about seven to ten percent of the snake's total length.

Coloration: Ground color is light gray, and patterned with about 60 black-bordered, brown dorsal blotches or spots between head and base of tail. On the dorsal line the blotches are separated by

76

areas of pale red, yellow, or orange. The tail usually has 12 or more spots. Ventral parts are light gray with brown or black blotches that extend upwards,

between the dorsal dark blotches. Black spots are usually present on the front part of the head, chin, and throat.

This snake, which seems to prefer high, dry pinelands, is a constrictor that feeds on small lizards and other snakes. When disturbed, it will vibrate its tail and strike at an intruder with a hissing sound. It is a secretive, burrowing snake that may be encountered under rocks, rotted stumps, fallen logs, loose bark, and forest debris.

Not much is known about this little snake; it is considered to be a rare species. However, they are known to be ovoviviparous in reproduction, and hatchlings are born with the same pattern as their parents.

Florida range: Records show that the species has been reported from Alachua, Citrus, Hernando, Pinellas, Marion, Seminole, Polk, Lake, and Orange counties.

The

Nonpoisonous

Snakes

Corn snake or red rat snake *Elaphe guttata guttata* (page 34). To a rat snake, breakfast is where you find it. If bird eggs are on the menu, it may take a bit of climbing. That's no problem for a rat snake; all are excellent climbers.

79

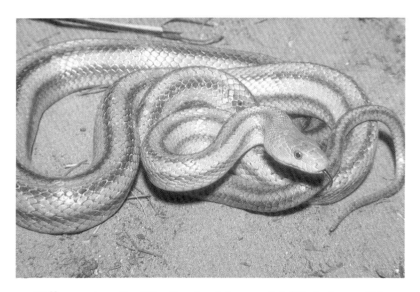

Yellow rat snake *Elaphe obsoleta quadrivittata* (page 37).

Yellow rat snake swallowing a mouse. Note the elasticity of the skin, and the unhinged jaw.

80

Gray rat snake *Elaphe obsoleta spiloides* (page 38).

Florida Pine Snake *Pituophis melanoleucus mugitus* (page 48).

Eastern kingsnake *Lampropeltis getulus getulus* (page 44).

Scarlet kingsnake *Lampropeltis triangulum elapsoides* (page 41).

Florida kingsnake *Lampropeltis getulus floridana* (page 45).

Florida scarlet snake *Cemophora coccinea* (page 46).

83

Black racer *Coluber constrictor priapus* (page 25).

Florida brown snake *Storeria dekayi victa* (page 74).

84

Southern hognose snake *Heterodon simus* (page 53).

This southern hognose snake continued to feign death as it floated belly-up on the surface of the water in a child's wading pool.

Skin shed of a snake's head. Note the eye cap that sloughed off with the skin.

This indigo snake *Drymarchon corais couperi* (page 28) had recently shed its skin, but the eye cap remained in place. Normally it is shed with the skin as in the top photo.

The snake that left this intact skin was aided in the shedding maneuver when it crawled over these sharp rocks and thorns.

A brown water snake *Nerodia taxispilota* (page 65) crawls away from its freshly shed skin. The skin at this point is quite soft and flexible, but in time it becomes hard and brittle.

Eastern coachwhip *Masticophis flagellum flagellum* (page 30).

A rough green snake *Opheodrys aestivus* (page 55) looks the situation over from the topmost branch of a tree.

Eastern garter snake *Thamnophis sirtalis sirtalis* (page 57) with young. They are probably very young indeed, because parent snakes do not stay around to provide any care to their offspring.

Eastern ribbon snake *Thamnophis sauritus* (page 57).

Mud snake *Farancia abacura* (page 71).

Banded water snake *Nerodia fasciata fasciata* (page 63).

POISONOUS SNAKES
(Venomous Snakes)

There are six species of dangerous, venomous snakes distributed throughout the Sunshine State. All share one feature: each is equipped with a pair of venom glands and a corresponding pair of long, hollow teeth (fangs) through which the venom is introduced into the wound that the snake inflicts on its victim.

Fangs are an exact reproduction, in enamel, of a hypodermic needle. Actually, it might be more appropriate to say that the person who invented hypodermic needles exactly duplicated the fangs of these reptiles; fangs have been around much longer than hypodermic needles!

Five of Florida's poisonous snakes (the pit vipers) have movable fangs. A single species (the coral snake) has erect, or rigid, fangs.

Most people today in Florida will likely live out their lives without ever encountering a single poisonous snake in the wild. But care should be taken (stay alert) when in the kind of habitat where such snakes exist. The bite of either of these six snakes (coral snake, copperhead, cottonmouth and three species of rattlesnakes) is extremely dangerous; they are reptiles TO BE AVOIDED!

The
Poisonous
Snakes

Head of eastern diamondback rattlesnake .

Eastern diamondback rattlesnake *Crotalus adamanteus* (page 110).

Canebrake rattlesnake *Crotalus horridus atricaudatus* (page 112).

Dusky pygmy rattlesnake *Sistrurus miliarius barbouri* (page 113).

96

Eastern coral snake *Micrurus fulvius fulvius* (page 101).

Cottonmouth *Agkistrodon piscivorous conanti* (page 107).

Cottonmouth juvenile.

Copperhead *Agkistrodon contortix contortix* (page 106).

Head of eastern coral snake.

BE CAREFUL when in copperhead country!

CORAL SNAKES

Many of the world's most poisonous snakes belong to the family Elapidae. The "asp" alleged to have caused the death of Cleopatra is believed to have been an Egyptian cobra, which is a member of this large family. Only two elapine snakes are found in North America, and fortunately for Florida residents, one of them (the Arizona coral snake) is alien to that state. The sole member in Florida is the eastern coral snake.

EASTERN CORAL SNAKE
Micrurus fulvius fulvius

A small snake with a black nape and a gaudy pattern of colorful rings encircling the body; average length is about two feet.

Coloration: The coral snake is easily recognized by the combination of a black nose, a pattern of rings of red, yellow, and black. The rings, unlike those of many other snakes, completely encircle the body. Scales are smooth, the head oval shaped (when observed from above), the snout short and rounded. Alternate broad black and broad red rings are separated by narrow yellow ones. The tail always lacks the red rings; it is simply black with broad yellow rings. The scales are smooth and glossy.

Despite its harmless appearance, the coral snake belongs to the family Elapidae, a family that includes some of the most deadly species of snakes in the world. Among the coral snake's close relatives are the cobras, mambas, kraits and the Australian tiger snake, all of which are noted for their resemblance to

THE CORAL SNAKE AND ITS MIMICS

SPECIES	RINGS	COLOR, PATTERN	BELLY	HEAD
CORAL SNAKE	Rings completely encircle the body. Tail lacks red rings.	Alternate broad black and broad red rings are separated by narrow yellow ones.	Rings extend across belly.	Head black with blunt snout.
FLORIDA SCARLET SNAKE	Rings do NOT encircle body – better described as "bands".	Narrow yellow bands, edged with narrow black ones, divide wide red bands.	No rings. Belly is white or yellow.	Head and pointed snout are red.
SCARLET KINGSNAKE	Rings encircle body. All three colors appear on tail.	Rings of the dorsal aspect appear very similar to bands of the scarlet snake.	Rings extend across belly but may be broken into blotches.	Head is red and pointed.

Both the Florida scarlet snake and the scarlet kingsnake resemble the deadly coral snake in color and pattern — no doubt a great asset for the two nonpoisonous species. All three species may inhabit the same area. The above chart may be helpful in differentiation.

harmless snakes. Though all possess very small fangs in comparison to those of the vipers, their venom glands are provided with venom that is more powerful than that of any living pit viper. The coral snake is no exception.

The coral snake's biting action is much like that of the cobras. Once they have seized the victim, they will advance the fangs into the flesh in a series of chewing motions. This kind of action can produce as many as four to eight separate, venom injected, punctures.

Unlike the movable fangs of the vipers, the two fangs of the coral snake are rigid and fixed to the front part of the upper jaw. They are solidly united to the maxillary bone, and directed backward at a permanent angle of about 45 degrees.

On the front surface of each fang is a distinct groove. In fact, these snakes have been described as possessing "grooved" fangs; this term is misleading and might give the novice the idea that the structure of the fang is like those of the rear-fanged snake group, Opisthoglyph. Although the face of the fang is deeply grooved, the venom-conducting teeth possess a hollow canal for the flow of venom and open in a small orifice at the tip, in the same fashion as a hypodermic needle.

The venom of the coral snake is neurotoxic, which means that it affects the nervous system of the victim, causing temporary paralysis and sometimes temporary blindness. Death is most often due to suffocation brought about by respiratory failure. Coral snake venom is the most toxic of all Florida snake venoms.

The coral snake is oviparous in reproduction. Its chalky white eggs are laid in decaying bark, or loose, damp soil and left to be incubated by the sun's radiation. The pattern of a hatchling is exactly like that of the parents, though some young individuals may display paler colors. The red rings may be a pale brick red color in the young. Hatchling are usually about seven inches in length, and can deliver a lethal dose of venom.

Coral snakes are especially fond of lizards, but will also feed on frogs and other snakes. All prey is seized and held in the mouth until dead, and then swallowed. The coral snake is a burrowing snake that is often accidentally turned up with a shovel in the loose soil of a garden, or when removing decayed logs, rocks, and debris.

Florida range: All of Florida, except for the extreme southern tip of the peninsula, where they rarely occur.

Habitat: Woodlands in general; perhaps most abundant around wooded lake margins.

PIT VIPERS – Family Viperidae

There are six species of pit vipers that are native to Florida. All are poisonous snakes belonging to the family Viperidae, subfamily Crotalinae. Not all members of that family are pit vipers, however; there are also some pitless vipers, none of which are found in the United States; most are half a world away in Europe, Asia, Australia and Africa. The missing pits, however, make them no less poisonous; they have the same dangerous apparatus, otherwise.

Pit vipers are so named for the small, deep, facial pit located on each side of the head, slightly below and midway between the eye and the nostril. This is a highly efficient temperature sensing device, so sensitive that a temperature difference of a fraction of a degree can be detected from some distance; this enables the snake to find warm-blooded prey, and to accomplish an accurate strike even in total darkness.

PIT VIPER
SIDE VIEW

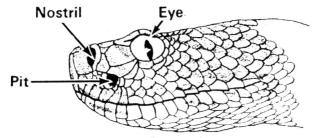

The pit viper's usual procedure is to strike, injecting its lethal venom, then to follow the victim until it dies and swallow it whole.

However, the snakes must have learned that birds have to be treated differently; when a bird manages to fly away before it succumbs to the poison, there is no trail for the snake to follow.

105

So the snake plays its safe and holds onto a bird until death occurs. Then it is swallowed.

All pit vipers have long, hollow, movable fangs, one on each side, located at the extreme anterior end of the upper jaw. The fangs are usually shed about every two weeks and replaced from a reserved series of new ones in the soft "gums" behind the active pair.

A bite from most pit vipers can be fatal to humans. The venom attacks the victim's circulatory system, dissolving blood cells and in most cases retarding clotting. Swelling and discoloration at and around the site of the bite is common, as is extreme pain. Anti-venom is available for most viper bites.

SOUTHERN COPPERHEAD
Agkistrodon contortrix contortrix

A heavy bodied, broad headed, medium-sized pit viper with broad, brown crossbands, with an average length of about two and a half feet. The neck is very distinct from the head.

Coloration: Ground color is very pale, including pastel shades of tan, buff, or pink. There are about 16 to 21 dark brown, hourglass shaped crossbands, some being so constricted in the middle that they fail to meet. Underparts are pale, with dark mottling. The top of the broad head is tinged with copper – hence the popular name. The upper lip may be a shade lighter than the head.

The copperhead is not an aggressive snake, but will not hesitate to defend itself when it is cornered. However, when threatened, the copperhead will first make an effort to escape. In defending itself, the snake rapidly vibrates its tail, which produces a distinct buzzing sound when the snake is on hard ground or dry leaves. The southern copperhead inhabits both dry and wet forest areas as well as open fields. During the heat of the day this snake may be encountered in tall grassy areas, under flat rocks, fallen logs, or wood piles. The copperhead's feeding habits usually change with the seasons. During the

106

spring and fall seasons it will live almost exclusively on frogs. During the late spring season it will add ground-nesting birds to its diet. During the summer months it seems to prefer small rodents. However, like all wildlife, the copperhead is an opportunist and will mix its daily diet when prey of the right size presents itself.

Ovoviviparous in reproduction, it gives birth to six or sometimes as many as nine young. These average about 10 inches in length and usually have a brilliant, sulphur-yellow colored tail, which, like the parents' tails, is vibrated when the young snake is disturbed. Like the parents, these youngsters are well camouflaged among dry leaves. Exercise extreme caution when hiking through forested areas and rocky hillsides in copperhead country!

Florida range: Known to be found in the Apalachicola drainage in Gadsen and Liberty counties.

Habitat: Hammocks and floodplain forests; fields.

COTTONMOUTH (Water Moccasin)
Agkistrodon piscivorus conanti

A thick bodied, broad-headed snake with a dark band on the side of the head, an abruptly tapered tail, and an average length of three feet. The facial pit between the eye and nostril identifies it as a member of the pit viper family.

Coloration: Pattern of 10 to 15 wide, dark crossbands on brown or olive brown ground color. Ventral parts are yellowish and mottled with a dark color. The side of the head has a broad, dark band running from the eye to the angle of the jaw. The upper lip plates are yellow. The top of the head is usually black or brown. Old specimens are sometimes almost uniformly black or brownish black with only a slight trace of the younger pattern described above; however, the head markings usually remain prominent.

The cottonmouth is a very irritable and pugnacious snake. When surprised by an intruder it will often draw its head back and up to face the intruder, opening its mouth wide to display the white mouth parts that earned it the name cottonmouth. It also vigorously vibrates the tail during such a threatening display. It will often strike out viciously at an intruder several times and then attempt an escape into the water which is part of its natural habitat.

Unlike most water snakes, the cottonmouth does not limit its food to cold-blooded prey, but it will feed on mammals and birds. Once the snake seizes the prey, it retains its hold, with fangs deeply imbedded, until the prey's struggling has ceased; only then does the swallowing process begin.

Ovoviviparous in reproduction, they give birth to 7 to 12 living young that average about 10 to 13 inches in length. The pattern of the newborn is vivid and quite different from that of the parents. They are brilliantly colored with a pale reddish brown background and bands of rich, dark brown. All bands and markings are narrowly edged with white. The young of this snake is often mistaken for a copperhead, another pit viper found in Florida.

Florida range: Found throughout all of Florida.

Habitat: Woodland ponds and tree-bordered marshes; rivers and swamps.

RATTLESNAKES
Genera Sistrurus and Crotalus

One group of pit vipers which is widely distributed throughout the United States is the rattlesnake. The outstanding characteristic of these snakes is the rattle. This is a loosely attached organ made up of horny segments which, when they make contact with one another, produce a buzzing sound when the tail is vibrated rapidly. These snakes vary in size, from

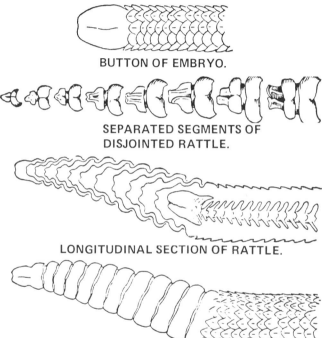

BUTTON OF EMBRYO.

SEPARATED SEGMENTS OF
DISJOINTED RATTLE.

LONGITUDINAL SECTION OF RATTLE.

PERFECT RATTLE, SIDE VIEW

small species reaching one and a half to two feet in length, to the eastern diamondback rattlesnake, known to reach over eight feet in length. The eastern diamondback is the largest of the poisonous snakes found in North America. There are 15 species of rattlesnakes distributed throughout the United States, which brings the total of poisonous snakes in this country to 19 species: two species of coral snakes, 15 species of rattlesnakes, the copperhead, and the cottonmouth.

All rattlesnakes are ground dwellers. None live in trees and none are burrowers. The main source of food for the rattlers includes rodents, rabbits, and birds; however, frogs, lizards, and other small creatures may also be added. Those rattlesnakes of the genus Sistrurus are all small species, one and a half to two feet in length, and can easily be identified by a group of nine uniformly large scales clustered together on the crown of the head. The larger species, of the genus Crotalus, have a mixture of large and small head scales. All rattlesnakes have a potent venom potentially lethal to humans.

The unique horny, segmented rattle is gained over a period of years. All rattlesnakes are ovoviviparous in reproduction, and all are born with a button. A new segment is added to this button each time the snake sheds its outer layer of dead skin – about three to four times per year. The maximum record of segments recorded in the wild was 24, in captivity, 30. Some people believe that the rattle is used as a warning to intruders, but this is pure speculation. The snakes themselves cannot hear the sound, at least not through air vibrations. There are many other snakes, some poisonous and some nonpoisonous, that also vibrate the tail rapidly when excited, but only the rattlers have rattles.

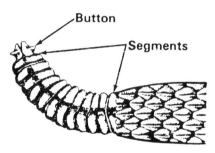

EASTERN DIAMONDBACK RATTLESNAKE
Crotalus adamanteus

A large, heavy rattlesnake with a dorsal pattern of diamond shaped markings and an average length of about four and one-half feet.

Coloration: Ground color brown or dusky, with 26 to 34 black or dark brown, diamond-shaped figures, wider than long, each lighter in the center and bordered by a row of light yellowish scales. Head is dark above, marked with light lines on the sides; nose plate (rostral) is usually edged with white. This snake is considered the largest North American poisonous snake, and one of the heaviest poisonous snakes in the world; record length is 98 inches.

This snake is considered by many herpetologists to be the deadliest of all North American poisonous snakes. This huge rattlesnake, with its brilliant and symmetrical markings is a beautiful and terrible creature, always bold and alert; there is a certain awe inspiring grandeur about the coil of this formidable reptile with the glittering black eyes, the slow-waving tongue, and the sound of the rattle. With all dignity, the diamondback often refuses to take cover when surprised.

Most rattlesnakes will usually retreat, rattling as they go, but retreating nonetheless – but not the diamondback. The mere vibration of a footstep puts this creature on guard. Inhaling deeply, the snake inflates its rough, scaly body with the sound of rushing air. Shifting its coils, it uncovers the rattle, which is immediately brought into play. There is no reckless striking, but careful watching until the opportune moment arrives. Only then – with incredible speed – will those long fangs deliver their accurate strike upon the intruder or prey – human or beast. If outstretched when surprised, the diamond-back invariably throws its body into a symmetrical coil, doubling the neck into an S-shaped loop with the head drawn well back and within the circle of the body. To observe a large specimen taken by surprise and see it literally fling itself into fighting position is to witness determination and courage that exists among very few reptiles.

Pine swamps and hammock lands are home to the diamondback rattlesnake. So closely do the body colors blend with the vegetation and the effect of sunlight and shadow, that the coiled snake is observed only with great difficulty. When moving in a leisurely fashion, it adopts the tactics characteristic

111

of poisonous snakes in general – slow progress in a perfectly straight line, with head slightly upraised.

The favorite food of the diamondback is the wild rabbit; however, other mammals, especially rodents of all descriptions, are also included in this snake's diet. The diamondback is ovoviviparous in reproduction, giving birth to from 7 to 12 young which feed readily on mice. Young grow rapidly, fully maturing in about two years.

Florida range: Found throughout the entire state.

Habitat: Widely distributed. Perhaps more abundant in open prairie with clumps of palmetto.

CANEBRAKE RATTLESNAKE
Crotalus horridus atricaudatus

A large, crossbanded rattlesnake with keeled scales and a pattern of dark crossbands on a lighter background, a mid-dorsal stripe on the forward part of the body, and an average length of about three and one-half feet; lengths above six feet have been recorded.

Coloration: Ground color is grayish brown to pinkish buff. Head has a conspicuous brown band that runs from the eye past the angle of the mouth. The dorsal area has a series of 23 to 32 dark blotches divided at the mid-line and more or less coming together at their outer edges. The side is marked by a series of narrow black streaks, alternating with another series of larger blotches along the lower side, and a very conspicuous mid-dorsal stripe which extends from nape to tail.

Because of the snake's preferred habitat (marshy lowlands, flatwood areas, and hammocks far from populated areas), humans seldom come in contact with the canebrake rattlesnake. The snake's diet consists of rabbits, rats, mice and birds. Not a very aggressive snake, it will attempt to escape whenever possible. However, when molested it will hold its ground, assuming a loose and irregular coil, and strike with great speed and accuracy. This snake has been known to turn from a crawling position, draw back the head by contracting the neck into an S-shaped loop, and deliver a quick, accurate, venomous bite – still quite uncoiled.

The canebrake rattlesnake gives birth to as many as twelve living young that measure 10 to 12 inches in length. In coloration they are much paler in color than the parents. Otherwise, the pattern is very much like that of mature specimens.

Florida range: Northern Florida southward to Alachua County.

Habitat: Flatwoods, river valleys and hammocks.

DUSKY PYGMY RATTLESNAKE
Sistrurus miliarius barbouri

A small, blotched, ill-tempered rattlesnake with minute rattles, which reaches an average length of about 18 inches. A little snake with large plates (instead of small scales) on top of the head. Scales are keeled.

Coloration: Ground color brownish gray on dorsal area. Pattern includes a median dorsal row of 27 to 45 dark spots and three lateral rows of smaller spots. A bright brown mid-dorsal stripes runs from nape backward, sometimes to the base of the tail. Ventral parts are light-colored, blotched with gray or black. The pygmy is the smallest of all living rattlesnakes. The head is flattened, and the neck very distinct. The rattle is tiny.

Because of the small size of the rattles, the sound of rattling can be heard for a distance of about eight feet, at most. The sound very much resembles that of a buzzing insect. However, it is a very offensive little rattler that will immediately coil and strike out vigorously at any intruder, large or small.

113

The pygmy rattlesnake frequents flatwoods and all kinds of dry and semi-dry environments close to small bodies of water and marshlands. Its favorite retreat is the burrow of the gopher tortoises or burrows made by rodents. Unlike most rattlesnakes, which feed exclusively on warm-blooded prey, the pygmy rattler is very fond of cold-blooded frogs, and will include them in its diet along with small rodents, newly hatched birds and small lizards.

Ovoviviparous in reproduction, the dusky pygmy rattlesnake produces six to ten living young that will measure about six inches in length. They will begin to feed almost immediately on insects and worms. Regardless of the size of the newborns and despite the small size of the fangs and venom glands, this snake should be highly respected.

Florida range: Inhabits the entire state.

Habitat: Flatwoods; most abundant near lakes and marshes.

CROWNED SNAKES (Rear-fanged snakes)
Genus *Tantilla*

All species of the genus Tantilla have fangs and venom glands and are therefore classified as poisonous snakes. However, unlike the coral snake and those snakes of the pit viper family which have their fangs positioned on the anterior part of the maxillary (upper jaw), the fangs of the crowned snakes are positioned at the posterior part of the jaw. There are five species of these diminutive reptiles that make their homes in Florida, but none are considered dangerous to humans. Their venom is comparatively mild and their tiny fangs too small to draw blood. The mild venom is capable only of subduing their proportionately small prey, which usually consists of centipedes, the larvae of insects that live underground, and an occasional tiny snake or lizard. Their fangs are not hollow, but are referred to as "grooved fangs'; the venom released from the venom gland flows down the groove and into the wound of the victim. The venom has a paralyzing effect on the prey, and serves to immobilize it, enabling the snake to swallow it more easily. They are very small both in length and girth. A specimen measuring nine inches in length will have a girth measurement of about nine-sixteenths of an inch. All the snakes of this genus live a very secretive life, spending most of their lives burrowing under loose soil, leaf mold, rocks, stones, and other objects not too deeply bedded in friable soil in open wooded areas and fields. Very rarely will any of these snakes exceed ten inches in length; the average length is about seven inches. A specimen of this size would have a tiny head that would measure no more than 7/32 of an inch.

To the casual observer, all species of crowned snakes are look-alikes. All are small, almost tiny, snakes with a slender body, brown to tan in color, with a black head followed by a narrow light line and a black collar. So closely do they resemble one another that it is almost impossible to properly identify either without a body scale count as well as a head scale count. All have somewhat flat heads, rather indistinct from the neck. As mentioned earlier, all have grooved fangs on the rear portion of the upper jaw, and do indeed produce venom, but may be classed among the reptiles innocuous to humans because their almost microscopic fangs would be unable to draw blood. For the reader to make positive identification of what crown snake is in hand (or being observed) refer to the artwork on scale and scale counting and identification on page 118. To help the reader, a drawing of the head of each species inhabiting Florida is shown with each outline of identification.

SOUTHEASTERN CROWNED SNAKE
Tantilla cornata

A tiny, tan snake with a black head, fifteen rows of smooth scales, and an undivided anal plate. Head lacks a loreal head scale, but has two internasal scales. Differs from the Florida subspecies described below in its higher ventral and subcaudal count and in the more well-defined light band on the back of the head. Average count of ventral plates in the males is 135, and those in the females of the species average 143. Subcaudal scales number 46 in male snakes, 44 in females. One preorbital scale in contact with postfrontals, which extend down to the labials. Upper labials number seven. Body is uniformly pale reddish brown to tan, with lighter ventral parts. The top of the head has a black cap bordered behind by a distinct light crossband that crosses the tips of the parietal scales and is bordered behind by a light black band on the nape; average length is about eight inches.

FLORIDA CROWNED SNAKE
Tantilla relicta neilli

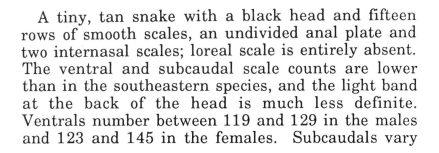

A tiny, tan snake with a black head and fifteen rows of smooth scales, an undivided anal plate and two internasal scales; loreal scale is entirely absent. The ventral and subcaudal scale counts are lower than in the southeastern species, and the light band at the back of the head is much less definite. Ventrals number between 119 and 129 in the males and 123 and 145 in the females. Subcaudals vary

116

from 50 to 67 in the males and from 41 to 59 in the females. Average length is about eight inches.

COASTAL PLAINS SNAKE
Tantilla relicta pamlica

This particular species has more white on its head than any other genus, and in addition to the light crossband there are usually light areas on the snout, the temporal and parietal scales (plates on the top of the head) as well as the posterior labials. The black collar is about three scales wide. Head is pointed; lower jaw is set deep into the upper. Dorsal area is reddish brown. Scales are smooth; anal plate is divided.

PENINSULA CROWNED SNAKE
Tantilla relicta relicta

Most of the head in this species is black, including labials. Very similar to the southeastern species, but this snake's crossband is often interrupted by black at midline; head is pointed and the lower jaw is partly set deep into the upper jaw, but not as deep as that of the southern crowned snake; scales are smooth, and the anal plate is divided.

RIM ROCK CROWNED SNAKE
Tantilla relicta oolitica

A crowned snake with an average length of about eight inches, and a head pattern that is very similar to that of the Florida species *Tantilla neilli*. Black on head continues from snout to neck; however, this same species occurs in Key Largo with a broken, light-colored crossband that separates the black head cap from the black collar. Scales are smooth, anal plate divided.

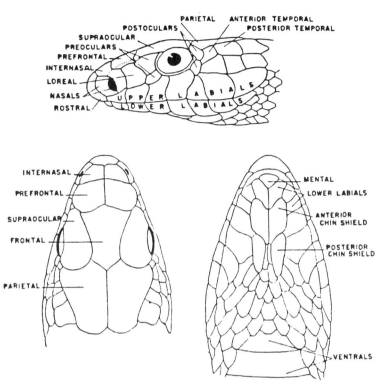

Lateral, dorsal and ventral views of head of snake, showing terminology of head scales.

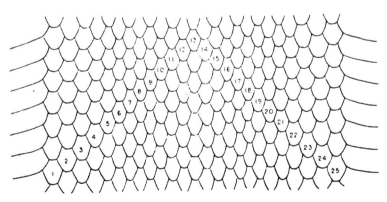

Method of counting rows of scales.

BIBLIOGRAPHY

Conant, Roger. *Reptiles and Amphibians of the Northeastern States*, third edition. Philadelphia: Zoological Society of Philadelphia, 1957.

Goin, Coleman J. and Olive B. Goin, *Introduction to Herpetology,* second edition. San Francisco: Freeman, 1971.

Harrison, Hal H. *The World of the Snake,* Philadelphia and New York: Lippicott, 1971.

Klauber, Lawrence M. *Rattlesnakes: Their Habits, Life Histories, and Influence on Mankind,* second edition, Berkeley and Los Angeles: University of California Press, 1972, two volumes.

Leviton, Allen E. *Reptiles and Amphibians of North America,* New York: Doubleday, 1972.

Pope, Clifford H. *The Reptile World,* New York: Knopf, 1955.

—. *Snakes and How They Live,* New York: Viking, 1957.

119

GLOSSARY

Abdomen   The belly region of vertebrates.

Anal   Pertaining to the anus.

Anal plate   The single or divided scale lying just in front of the anus of a reptile.

Anatomy   The structure of a living organism.

Anterior   Head or front end of the body of an animal.

Antibody   A substance in the blood that combats harmful toxins or bacteria.

Antiseptic   A substance that retards or prevents the growth of disease-producing bacteria.

Antitoxin   A serum, the antibodies of which neutralize the toxin given off by disease-producing bacteria or venom received in the bite of a poisonous snake.

Antivenin   A serum used in treating the bite of a venomous reptile.

Antivenom   A serum extracted from a horse that has been injected with the venom of a poisonous reptile.

Anus   The opening at the lower end of the alimentary canal.

Aquatic   Living in water.

Arboreal   Living in trees.

Behavior   The manner in which an organism acts or responds.

Biology   The science of life, including the study of the development, structure, and the behavior of living organisms.

Brackish   Water which is a mix of fresh and salt water.

Carnivore	A living organism that feeds on the flesh of other animals.
Cartilage	A tough, elastic tissue in animals, sometimes called gristle.
Caudal	Pertaining to the tail.
Constrictor	A snake that subdues its prey by squeezing it to death.
Convulsion	A violent, involuntary contraction or spasm of the muscles.
Digestion	The sum total of the processes by which foods are converted into usable form.
Diurnal	Active during the daytime. (Antonym: nocturnal.)
Dorsal	The upper surface, or back, of an organism.
Ecology	A study of the relation of organisms to their environment.
Ecosystem	A system formed by the interaction of a community or organisms with their environment.
Ectothermic	Cold-blooded, i.e. one whose body temperature is determined by the temperature of the surrounding environment. (Antonyms are endothermic, homoiothermic, and warm-blooded.)
Elliptical	Having the form of an ellipse or oval, like a cat's eye or the eye of snakes in the viper family.
Envenom	To make poisonous.
External ear opening	The ear canal that leads to the outside of an animal's head.

Extremities	The outermost parts which extend outward from an organism's main body: arms, legs, tail, etc.
Fang	A hollow or grooved tooth through which poison flows from the venom gland into the bite wound.
Forage	To search for food.
Gland	An organ of secretion or excretion: e.g., a sweat, oil or venom gland.
Habit	Characteristic mode of behavior.
Habitat	Typical environment in which an animal lives.
Haemotoxin	A poison capable of attacking and destroying red blood cells in both warm and cold-blooded animals. Often applied to poisons that cause hemorrhaging.
Immobilize	To make motionless.
Infection	A disease caused by the presence in the body, of toxic microorganisms.
Inflict	To impose something damaging or painful.
Inject	Introduce or force a fluid or other substance into body tissues, as with a hypodermic needle or a poisonous reptile's fang.
Intergrade	Overlapping areas of different species' territory.
Keel	Longitudinal ridge.
Laceration	Cut or scrape that breaks through the surface of the skin.
Labials	The lip plates of reptiles.
Locomotion	The process of moving from one place to another.

123

Loreal pit	The deep depression on the sides of the head, between the nostril and the eye in the loreal region, which is present in the pit vipers.
Marsh	A tract of soft land that grows tall grasses.
Median	Middle line.
Neurotoxin	A poisonous substance which attacks the nervous system.
Nocturnal	Active during the nighttime. (Antonym: diurnal)
Organism	Any living animal or plant.
Ovary	The organ of a plant or animal which produces eggs.
Oviparous	Producing eggs from which the young are hatched outside the body.
Ovoviviparous	Producing living young, which have developed within the mother's body from eggs (no placental attachment).
Paralysis	Loss of the ability to move or to feel, in part or all of the body of a living organism.
Pit	See loreal pit.
Placenta	The vascular organ in mammals that unites the fetus to the maternal womb, through which the fetus receives nourishment.
Poisonous	Describing a living organism whose bite or sting releases a toxic substance which can cause illness or death.
Posterior	Pertaining to the rear part.
Prey	Animals which are hunted and killed by other animals for food.
Protein	Any of the class of complex nitrogenous substances which occur in living matter.

Pugnacious	Of a fighting attitude; quarrelsome.
Puncture	A hole made by a sharp, pointed instrument; the piercing of the skin with such an instrument.
Pupil	The contractile circular opening in the center of the iris of the eye.
Radiation	The rays sent out by the sun; ultraviolet rays for light and infrared rays for warmth.
Rodent	A mammal of the order Rodentia, which includes small, gnawing animals.
Rostral	Pertaining to the rostrum.
Rostrum	A beak or snout.
Salt marsh	Flat land subject to overflow by salt water.
Scalation	The arrangement and character of scales.
Scale	Any of the flat, horny plates covering reptiles, fish, some mammals, and the legs and feet of birds.
Scute	An external bony or horny plate or large scale.
Segment	Any of the parts into which something is separated; the rattle of a rattlesnake is made up of segments.
Semi-aquatic	Living part of the time in the water.
Septicaemia	Invasion of the bloodstream by virulent organisms.
Species	A division of a genus
Specimen	An individual member which exemplifies a whole or group.
Suffocate	To kill by cutting of air for breathing; asphyxiate.

125

Swamp	An area of soft, spongy land which holds water.
Swelling	An increase in size due to an accumulation of fluid.
Symptom	A condition which indicates the presence of a health problem.
Temporal	Pertaining to the sides of the skull, posterior to the eyes.
Terrestrial	Living on the ground.
Toxic	Poisonous.
Trunk	The body, not including the head or limbs. In snakes, the head and tail are not included.
Ventral	Pertaining to the belly or underparts of an organism.
Viscera	The organs in the body cavity of an animal: heart, lungs, and intestines, for example.
Viviparous	Producing live young which have developed within the mother's body, nourished through a placenta. (Also sometimes used as a general term to include ovoviviparous development.)

INDEX

Boldface page numbers indicate color illustrations.

128